Babes on Blades

Drop Physical, Mental and Spiritual Flab
Through Inline Skating

Suzan Davis

Wish Publishing
Terre Haute, Indiana
www.wishpublishing.com

LCCN: 2001099361

Proofread by Heather Lowhorn
Editorial assitance provided by Natalie Chambers
Cover designed by Phil Velikan
Cover photography by Joe Ajax
Photography credits for interior are listed on page

Printed in the United States of America
10 9 8 7 6 5 4 3 2 1

Published in the United States by
Wish Publishing
P.O. Box 10337
Terre Haute, IN 47801, USA
www.wishpublishing.com

Distributed in the United States by
Cardinal Publishers Group
7301 Georgetown Road, Suite 118
Indianapolis, Indiana 46268
www.cardinalpub.com

To Betty and Al
I'll never forget you.

Sometimes Wee-Babes aren't much bigger than their gear.

Table of Contents

It's always important to put safety first.
"Helmet head" is what they say. Joke's on them; it hides the gray...
at least until it falls out.

Acknowledgements

When the skating bug bit me in the buns back in 1995, all kinds of you-know-what broke loose and an unanticipated journey began. I traded a diminished self for a renewed spirit. I thank those who supported my endeavors and encouraged me as I blazed new territory in trying to inspire a previously ignored audience—women over forty—who were not necessarily active in the first place.

I thank Dennis, Katelyn and Savannah Neary for their unending support and participation in my antics, as well as Brian Snelson, editors Nancy Ackley, Kathy Gire, Claudine Fall and Kate Lang. Also, Dr. Elizabeth "Da Winch" Taylor for insisting I put a little "F" (fun) on my calendar plus obtain a Master's Degree, a twenty-five-year-old dream. To Dr. Dahling Marlene Von Fredricks Fitzwater for her advice when I went back to school after all those years. Her advice rings true in all endeavors: "You don't have to be the best, you don't have to be the brightest, you just need to be the one that does not give up. No matter what, don't quit."

To all the Babes—especially the original three hundred Roseville members, many whom remain friends today like Babe Pat Musselman and Babe Sandy Adsit, who carried the Babe Message across the nation, plus Babe Kathy Reusch and Babe Kathy S., remarkable He-Babes Mark Richards and Terry Dent, and hairy He-Babe Mike, plus so many others who donned the Babe shirt and acted as if they owned the world for two and a half hours every Saturday, and encouraged the innocent public to join in. Thank you He-Babe Ron Williams for helping me get hundreds of people over fifty on skates for the first time, over the past half dozen years.

To David Miles who created Napa to Calistoga and other avenues for skaters, regardless of skill level. Along with his wife Rose,

David cheered me on from the beginning, the only participant in his skate race who showed up in pink maternity golf shorts.

I thank Alicia Keller of the Sporting Goods Manufacturers Association (SGMA) and Maria Stephans also of the SGMA, for seeing the potential that Babes have to inspire desire and fire in others to experience exercise, and for flying Babes to Atlanta and New York to do just that.

To Captain John Butterfield, SGMA, formerly IISA, for shaping the Babes in their early days by insisting they always wear helmets—rarely done by existing skaters in those days. Most refused to join Babes for that reason. Captain John said it was easier to sell new skaters on the idea of wearing safety gear than experienced ones, which proved to be true. When Captain John called me from across the country, his enthusiastic tone gave me a shot in the arm that had been missing. Acknowledgment of something I had accomplished had not happened since the birth of my first child, five years earlier. His friendship and support means a great deal to me.

I thank my early editors who ran my column with my picture, Jeff Caraska of *the Roseville Press Tribune*, Nadine Brown of *Global Skate* and Reggie Winner of *California Hockey and Skating*.

To Babe Kathy Reusch for her photography and artistic renditions and Renelle Mare for editing my master's thesis plus this book. To Dr. Peter Boyum for enduring the "Babe grammar olympics." And last but not least Babe Dawn, the Babe of Babes who caught the Babe Buzz, edited this book from top to bottom, and picked up and now carries the Babe Torch to another generation.

Part One
Be a Babe

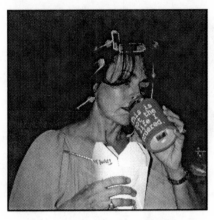

Take one tired woman

Put skates on her

Voila! A Babe on Blades

Reclaim Your Babe Within

The time is now to challenge the unrealistic, out-dated definition of a Babe. A Babe is not some young female starved for attention, not to mention ice cream. Babes need not bare size-two thighs. Take this vision and let testosterone bearers embrace it while you erase it. Rip this image of a Babe out of your mind and put your wondrous self in the picture instead.

Although you may not feel like a Babe at the moment, trust me, there is one deep within you. Reclaim her. This book jumpstarts your motor into Babe overdrive. Go ahead, you deserve it; you're a Babe.

This is a hungry woman
(obviously!)

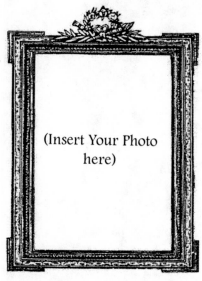

(Insert Your Photo here)

This is a *Babe*

Who is a Babe?

You are a Babe. At least you have the potential. For the most part, a Babe is primarily a woman with the weight of the world on her shoulders and a little of that has spread over her body. She needs an escape from the insanity caused by work, family, and life in general. When you take this stressed animal and put inline skates on her, something happens. Something good. She begins to sashay and glide from side to side. As the breeze sweeps over her brow, she begins to forget the chores that lie ahead. Thoughts of the cleaning, the cooking, and the million pressures of a woman's complex world are replaced by other ideas. These include traveling forward, instead of flying up into the air or plopping onto the ground. Babes do not like to land on their heinies, but they risk it, banking on the adrenaline charge that lies ahead—if they just do it. They enjoy the tightening of physical and mental flab, the increased sense of pride, and the release of the Babe within. Take a tired woman, put skates on her feet and soon after she morphs into a Babe on Blades.

Babes have sass

Babes are playful

☞ Babeisms ☜

Babes enjoy a number of sayings that serve them well, and Babes serve them often: Practice these daily until you reek this attitude. It will get you far. Why? Because you are a Babe.

- I am a Babe. Who says? I do.
- *What makes a Babe a Babe?* I am a Babe because I say so.
- Do it my way, or get out of my way. *(For bossy Babes)*
- I feel so good, I feel like a Babe.
- I deserve it. It's my turn now.
- If you feel guilty, you are not a Babe.
- Babes not only deserve treats, they demand them.

- Babes come in all sizes from 2 to size 2XXX. We roll our rolls, taking what we have, making it better.
- I can get away with it. I am a Babe.
- Babes don't worry about fat — we like you just the way you are.
- Babes try to stay out of trouble, but make no promises.
- Babes get what they want, when they want it.

Babes have
attitude empowerment

Babes have a
special view of the world

No, I wasn't always the Babe you see before you.

2

The Beginning

HOW THE WHOLE BABE THING GOT STARTED
a Personal Journey

The squawking sounds of my children made it difficult for me to hear his soft words. I leaned forward placing my elbows on the cold tile and asked him to repeat them. As I did, my nostrils filled with the smell of Comet® radiating from my hangnails. I glanced around my kitchen. Shoes and socks recklessly torn off tiny feet were spread on the linoleum. Dolls and toys had been plopped on the counter top, clear only moments before. Remains of a spilled bag of potato chips were crushed into a trail leading nowhere, everywhere, highlighted by Popsicle footprints. A woman with a bad hairdo stared back at me in the reflection off the microwave oven door. There was my face between splatters of exploded baby food.

"You ought to do this; it'd be good for you." His finger pointed to an ad in an inline skating magazine, a publication I previously ignored because its pages were filled with wildly fit people committing acts that defied gravity. My magazine collection addresses iron-poor blood and the horrors of leaky diapers in public places. The announcement he spoke of was for a twenty-seven-mile skate race from Napa to Calistoga, California. My mind did a somersault. When it landed, I knew if I looked up, my kitchen would be clean, the children grown and earning money, and I would be slimmer and taller. I was having my first bona fide hallucination.

The man was Brian Snelson, a representative for K2 Corporation, manufacturer of skis, snowboards and inline skates. The latter are like roller skates but have four wheels in a row, or in a line. They are sometimes called Rollerblades®, the way gelatin is called Jell-

O®. Brian and I met after an article appeared in his hometown Sunday newspaper about my friends' and my discovering the fun of inline skating, *rediscovering* our inner juveniles and our hopes of skating across the country. It was not the plausibility of our mission that intrigued him, it was our ages.

He got my name from the newspaper and arranged to meet me in a community college parking lot saying he wanted to give me a free pair of skates with *five* wheels. It was cold and drizzly on our scheduled meeting date, leaving the parking lot wet and slippery. Brian held out a box. "Fed Ex delivered these today," he said, opening it.

He extracted a pair of yellow and black K2 Extreme Workouts with five wheels from a large box labeled "Next Day Service." They looked wild—like gigantic yellow and black bumblebees with wheels. "Here, take them. Since you are going to get famous, do it in these." Brian explained that the Babes on Blades represented an untapped segment of the market that skate manufacturers wanted to reach—the over thirty-five women's market. I did not know what he was talking about, but felt pretty grand to receive an athletic product, especially since I had never participated in organized sports, was considered overweight, and was a closet smoker.

A sudden, unexplainable sense of burden intermingled with excitement overcame me.

"Let's see you on them," he said, yanking crumpled paper out of the skates before pulling off my loafers. I regretted wearing thick, wool socks; a big toe poked through one of the holes at the end. Brian placed the skates on my feet, wrenching them up and lacing them tight. In a state of disbelief, or shock, I tried to take it all in sitting right there on the floor of his van with my legs dangling out the side door. I felt anchored by the skates; the additional wheel made them long and awkward. Brian grabbed a hand and pulled me up.

"Time to skate," he said.

Scrambling in place like a doe on ice, I attempted to look as if skating were effortless for me. Impossible. The pavement was slippery from the rain and I could not get my footing. Still, I managed not to fall; an image of grace I was not.

"You can't skate worth beans, but it doesn't matter," he said.

"I'll drop by in a few days to see how you are doing."

Now he was in my kitchen making that ridiculous suggestion about the Napa race. I had only been skating eight weeks. Though the sport had created a whole new improved me, I could think of dozens of reasons this mission would not be possible. *Twenty-seven miles.* At nearly forty, my thighs rubbed together when I walked. What would happen when I skated that distance—spontaneous combustion? A fire in my pants?

I pictured my initial attempts at skating. Traveling with my arms outstretched, legs wide apart, I glided along pavement powered by a force I could not see. That force was under feet that were holding generous poundage upon a mere five-foot-two-inch frame. It got a lot of laughs from the neighbors. My two- and four-year-old daughters, Katelyn and Savannah, caught in the moment, joined the adults with fits of laugher. A sassy neighbor in his seventies bellowed from the window of his old pickup truck: "No old ladies on roller skates."

"The race is next Saturday," Brian said, jolting me back to the present.

It was a matter of mind over body. Wait, make that mind over mind—the planning mind, the doubting mind, the practical mind, the worrisome mind vs. the dreaming mind—my mind.

His were the comments of a free man made to a domestically enslaved woman. I resented that. I had too many roadblocks to overcome such as finding a baby sitter, my physical conditioning—or lack there of—fear of blisters, lack of technique and skill, to name a few. Napa was 100 miles away. I was not used to traveling beyond the property line unless it was to skate the two-mile stretch of road in front of my house or make a diaper run by car. He was suggesting I do something that in the past I would have never considered because I was not at my "ideal weight"—something I had not seen since age ten. Forget him.

I started to think about the people who would attend the Napa to Calistoga skate race. There probably would be women possessing bodies tighter than over-stretched rubber bands and men young enough to be my children. These were people from a different world— folks taut, free, hopping high, and coming up from falls as if the concrete had springs. My idea of experiencing a fall resulted in getting x-rays immediately. I do not relish the thought of what happens after gravity turns the pavement against me. This one was for someone else. No way would I consider it.

Five days later I was in Napa checking into a motel that had the word "budget" in a big sign in the parking lot boasting "$39.95!" The word meant just that, a place operating on a budget. It was more of a warning, rather than a promise. I still had doubts about the whole thing—nagging, relentless doubts.

The dimly lit hotel was on the outskirts of town. A bunch of strangers hung around the parking lot. Casually dressed, some milled about holding cans of cheap beer and speaking to no one in particular. I wondered why they were there. Didn't they have some place to go? The following morning I awoke to Dennis, my husband, saying, "Wake up. All those people you were afraid of last night are waiting for you at the registration table. They are the support team."

After registering, I shook my head in wonder. Athletes surrounded me. Why had I listened to Snelson? Why did he think I could do something that *real athletes* do? He dealt with them on a regular basis. He *had* to notice I was not built like one but more like two! What did he see in me that I could not?

I studied the crowd. They were dressed in brightly colored, skin-tight outfits wrinkle-free from neck to knee. I donned my pink maternity golf shorts from three summers before and a shirt denoting a sassy woman on inline skates boasting, "**Caution! Babes on Blades.**" I felt brave to wear it. Did anyone else here sag under the arms? My self-image did not fit this picture. Perhaps I needed to change it.

A big voice came over a loud speaker, "Welcome to the sixth annual Napa to Calistoga Skate Race. Make sure the numbers in your registration packets are visible. Pin them to your right pant leg. In three minutes, we will proceed to the starting point. Stick together and go two miles down Main, then turn left on Silverado. Stop at all red lights or risk a ticket. The friendly Napa Police Department will escort us."

A dazzlingly array of colorful man/womankind took off through the sleeping town. I gathered up my self-doubts and started to trudge forth in the black and yellow skates. Brian had mentioned that the fifth wheel provides an additional twenty percent of glide off each push, compared to four-wheelers. Too occupied to feel excited about this advantage, I studied the ground directly under my feet, watching for scattered sticks, gravel, sand, water, uneven pavement and other road terrors. I plowed into the person ahead, almost knocking both of us over.

"Your skates follow what your eyes see," a smiling woman, also in her late thirties, offered. "Look at the ground—end up on the ground. Look forward—roll forward. It really works; you'll see."

With a charming smile, she glided safely out my way.

Dennis followed in our ten-year-old Plymouth Voyager. The other skaters were incredibly calm. Some chatted and even laughed. A slender fellow in his twenties casually sipped coffee as he rolled along. I wondered when the urinary consequences of caffeine would hit him. What would he do then?

Enveloped by a sea of bright fabrics, I did my best to keep up with the other skaters. I did not want to be left behind. The idea was terrifying. The names of skate teams and advertisers were splashed all over shirts and skin suits. Made of stretchy material, most had expandable pockets placed on the bottom center of the back, with three pockets sewed in a row. The middle pocket usually had a water bottle poking out with an occasional banana peeking from a side one. Other skaters wore T-shirts from previous sporting events over dark spandex pants.

The group made a wide left and suddenly stopped. We were at the race's official starting point though I almost missed it, too busy studying the array of butts immediately in front of me. I could not hear the last minute rules about skating on the right side of the road, or where to gather after the race. I busily sized up the other racers, hoping to find one that looked as slow as I felt. What were they thinking behind their sunglasses?

The whistle sounded. Eighty skaters dashed up the winding road. In a pack, they leaned in unison, taking on a curve ahead. Just like that, they were gone. It was now just the novice skaters—or "citizen class." What a relief! There must have been at least forty people left with me. I started to glide, making small pokes at the pavement. It took a while to get out of my thoughts and into my feet. Someone was closing in. A little boy, about eight, passed me. The first of many.

I tried hard to concentrate on the road and put one skate in front of the other without so much effort. I looked for the van, but did not see it. I was struggling and the race had just begun.

About ten long minutes into the event, it occurred to me that of all people, *I* was there with *them*. These were people who show up, get out of the house, take risks and in this case, participate in a sporting event. Some competed for money; others did it just for fun. So far, it had not been too fun, though suddenly, it was a bit of a thrill. This feeling was completely unexpected. My skates fell into a rhythm and the soothing sound of the wheels' hum rose up from the pavement. The distance ahead was overwhelming, so I purposely took notice of the scenery. Thousands of rows of grapes led to winery after winery. I had never been to Napa. I did not know it then, but it was the first of many times my skates would lead me to new and exciting places, some close to home but worlds away mentally.

The asphalt unfolded smoothly, but my thoughts were still rocky. I was afraid of hills, running out of water, tripping on roadkill, getting hit by a car, and being left miles and miles behind. You name it and it would eventually fall into my "fear think." I consider myself an expert in worrying about that which other people forget to lose sleep over. I skated. And skated. And skated some more.

As I came to a hill's crest, I startled a cow that had wandered from her pasture to graze on the side of the road, just behind a sharp turn. Face to face with a cow! I looked at her. She looked at me. I looked at her. She did not let up her gaze. When I finally took my eyes off the cow, it was too late; I was zooming down the hill. Instead of going with the flow of the road, which eventually evened out, I panicked and fell, landing on the yellow line on the middle of the highway. I did not linger, popped up and rolled the rest of the way down, having learned that she who tries to outstare a cow loses.

I knew I was skating farther than ever before. At times other participants would pass, other times, though not often, I would come across someone and pass him or her. Spread out over the course, we were held together by a common bond—and I was a part of the bond of a team for the first time in my life. Determined not to quit, my biggest roadblock I realized, was not my feet; it was my mind. The fear of the unknown bore more weight than any reality. A long list of anxieties melted away as I glided forward.

There was Dennis, up the road, with the old Instamatic camera. Holding up four fingers, he wore a **HUGE** smile. I knew what he meant—four more miles! I was going to make it!

"Four miles to go!" I verified with a victorious shout.

"No. Twenty-three miles to go. You've *gone* four."

Twenty-three miles later I crossed the finish line, passing a group of wildly cheering people. I knew they were blown away by my life-affirming accomplishment. They were. They were also glad to finally see the last of the skaters so they could pack up and join the rest of the group of 109, at the park for lunch.

I was ecstatic! I did it! I wanted to scream. I wanted to cry. Only five days earlier I deemed this quest impossible. I had put on my skates and conquered the great unknown. I had done Napa to Calistoga. It was the best I had felt in years.

I caught up with three others and skated through the town of Calistoga to reach the park. People paused to observe us. Outside diners looked up from their breakfasts and asked each other who "those people" were. As we maneuvered the sidewalks and curbs, we heard more than once: "Look! Who are they? Must be racers. Maybe they're making a movie." That was my favorite. I was proud to be among the skaters. I was renewed. The music in my ears was no longer the whirl of the washer and dryer but the rhythmic rolling of skate wheels.

Later that evening, glowing with supercharged self-confidence, I skated fifteen miles in my own neighborhood. I had journeyed beyond my own thinking. I felt like the confident woman on my T-shirt. I indeed was a "Babe on Blades."

As I lay in bed that night with Band-Aids® covering my blisters and the girls tucked in for the night, I could not help but remember how this all started with the ring of the doorbell months earlier. There stood my thirty-nine-year-old pal Nancy.

"Want to go rollerblading?" she asked innocently.

I looked at her as if she had swallowed a bee. Nancy is a nurse and seemingly sane, but I wisely refused. I had seen those skate-things before. Wildly aggressive youths jump off stairs and hand rails with them. Inlines looked very dangerous, indeed, providing entertainment only for the young and reckless. I grouped them with the skateboarders one finds jumping off curbs in busy parking lots. Initially, you hope they do not wipe you, your newborn and your grocery cart off the face of the earth. Later, you hope you don't hit them with *your* car but wish someone else would. To me, street skaters of any kind were a menace to society. Period.

Nancy came over the next day with the same question and got the same answer. I had spent the three-day weekend trying to keep our two- and four-year-old daughters out of Dennis' way while he and three friends worked on an addition to the garage. Laughing continuously while listening to baseball games, drinking beer, and enjoying what we females call "male bonding," he would have something permanent to show for his time. I had applause-worthy clean and folded laundry plus trophy-deserving scrubbed toilets that would demand attention again within mere days. Curiously, this did not fulfill—much less nurture—the spirit within.

I let out a long sigh after sending Nancy home. Dennis looked at me, utterly disgusted. With his brows squinted into a knot he asked, *"Why do you look so tired all the time? All you do is watch children!"*

"Where are those skates we bought three years ago that I never wore?" I responded. I blew a generous layer of dust off the box, put them on, and *was out the door.*

Nancy and I collected another friend, Stephanie, and the three of us were soon rolling and laughing like teenagers. The next day and the day after, and for the next six weeks, we could hardly wait each day to abandon our kitchens and head for the road. We had become addicted to having something to look forward to while acting as foolish as our own children. We noted the changes in us— tighter tushes and wildly optimistic thinking replaced sagging minds and buns. Since the Olympics was going to be in Atlanta later that year, we talked about skating all the way to Chicago to meet Oprah. Then we would roll with her to the Olympics. We had moved from small-town thinking to global dreaming. The skates truly had affected our minds in an upbeat and optimistic way. Stephanie suggested we have shirts made that said, *"Moms on Blades."*

I shot back without even thinking about it, "I feel so good, I feel like a Babe." From then on, we were the Babes on Blades.

We began to plan our trek across the country. After some consideration—about ten seconds worth—we realized we needed an RV to get us over the rough spots. I decided to contact the Recreation Vehicle Industry Association (RVIA), and ask if they would lend us an RV so that we could have a "hotel on wheels," plus bring our families on our remarkable journey. My parents and I had been lobbyists for RVIA years before. I knew it would be good exposure for both inline skating and the recreation vehicle industry. I dialed the phone with confidence.

"How do I know you'll get any publicity?" The gentleman on the other line asked. It was a question that changed my life. "Could you please send me a press release?"

I had never written one, but did as he asked. While at it, I faxed the release to several newspapers and television stations. For the press release, see the following page.

Within days the three of us were featured in a widely circulated newspaper insert called "Neighbors." It pictured our smiling faces exuding our newfound gusto along with shots of us skating past a duck pond, hooting all the way. I hoped the article would generate sponsors to assist our trek. What happened was quite different. Seven out of eight papers that got the press release either ran a story on us or simply printed the release as written, with photos. Each bit of publicity brought calls asking how to join the club. Club? There was no club to join.

Four weeks after the Napa race, Dennis asked me what I wanted to do for my fortieth birthday. It was looming on the horizon like a dark cloud on a sunny day. I pictured a dozen black roses and a cake with a tombstone candle lurking in the frosting. "I want to skate," I answered.

"Then do it," he said. "Have a skating party."

I wondered how I would find people to accompany me.

Dennis said, "Do what you do best. Invite the whole world and introduce yourself to whoever shows up." I put out press releases inviting the public to join me as I "faced the official ending of my youth, sex appeal and who-knows-what" by skating my age—40—one kilometer at a time. I asked Brian if K2 Corporation would pro-

FOR IMMEDIATE RELEASE...
Contact: Suzan Davis, (555)555-9000

Having an overwhelming need to feel the wind against their dish pan hands, three mothers, whose children range in age from two to twenty-two, swiped some inline skates one day and escaped to the street. Accepting the challenge of staying up, and wobbling zestfully, this unlikely group of out-of-shape, unspectacular, nonathletes were shocked at what they discovered. It was *big fun*. And they could do it! And they have kept doing it.

After many years of high-speed diaper changes, tackling all manner of stains, and picking laundry off just about everything, these middle-aged women realized there was something missing in their lives but could not figure out what it was. They no longer saw themselves as "Sweet Young Things" but more like caged animals with no place to run. The gym was too inconvenient and expensive. When one signed up, she went three times and quit—lamenting the money she was spending while she grew fatter, not firmer. Seeing her reflection in a mirror with the dazzling spandex-laden lassies hopping and popping around her she went home feeling defeated. Like a cow, she returned to her pasture. Another mom threw herself into a strict diet only to find her thoughts constantly on food, which resulted in rampages—scattering the family in all directions as they sought to escape her snapping dishtowel. Another mom worked full-time in an office to come home to her other full-time job—her family. She too needed a way to relieve stress, but how?

— MORE —

Then they discovered "*the blade.*" They planned to do it only once but immediately realized, **once was not enough**. Enduring laughs and jeers shouted from car windows and neighborhood front yards, they strapped on their skates at every opportunity and rolled forth. Ever fearful of smacking the pavement with their faces, they proceeded with safety gear firmly in place. Soon they became respected for their gusto and cheered forward.

Many former critics and finger-pointers now stand along the street and root them on. Countless others are trying it themselves. The physical benefits are remarkable and unexpected. These skaters feel calmer in calamity, their bodies are firming up, and they all experience a new sense of confidence which stays with them as they deal with the events of the day plus occasional situations that not long ago made them cower and retreat. They were too tired for confrontation. Not any more.

They decided to name themselves "Moms on Blades," but this suddenly sounded too old for these thirty- and forty-something gals. Thus, "Babes on Blades" was born. They sport tee shirts that say just that while denoting three inline skaters in various stages of "flight."

A former heckler was caught one evening inline skating for the first time and confessed, "I've been on these things for fifteen minutes and I see why they do it; it makes you high!"

That's right America! Feel the adrenaline, the rush, the high—it's as close as your feet and it has healthy side effects. Watch out! Skating causes untold energy that continues long after the skates are taken off. Chores are tackled with gusto, the children are scolded less, and their husbands are feeling lucky tonight.

These bodacious Babes convey to others the benefits of this unlikely but healthy alternative to a mid-life crisis. They show other moms, plus dads, that they too have playgrounds as close as the end of their driveways. They plan to spread this message across the planet. This venture is not always cheap or easy, but neither are the "Babes on Blades."

— END —

vide free use of skates and safety equipment for folks who did not have their own. They did. Three weeks after Dennis' skate party suggestion, one hundred people I did not know and a handful of friends showed up at 7 o'clock—when most decent people are asleep on a Saturday morning.

The Babes on Blades became an official inline skating club that day. Eight new members signed up and got a shirt and a newsletter. Everyone got a piece of birthday cake. Two hundred and fifty others joined within six months. We began making regular television, radio, and paid guest appearances at special events and expositions, promoting self-esteem through this physical outlet for women, men and children.

"Why don't you write a column about skating?" a friend blurted out one day. "That way you can get the word out without rounding up the press all the time. Stop calling the press. *Be* the press."

"Impossible," I retorted. "I know nothing about writing newspaper columns."

"If you can learn how to skate, you can learn how to write a newspaper column. I'll give you three weeks."

Four weeks later the "Babes on Blades" column appeared in the local newspaper, the *Roseville Press Tribune*. It included my mugshot. A few months later, I was introduced at an event for newspaper writers as the only columnist who wears a helmet over her by-line.

Again, skating took me out of the box, beyond my invisible limits. It opened my mind to the unexplored and enabled me to hear my friend's words and put them into action. I had never thought about writing a column until someone told me to *just do it*. The column has been published to date in ninety countries in newspapers, sports magazines, and national and international publications. Naturally, it is about the thrills of participating in skating escapades and even races, be it alone, with another person, or in large groups. Only one person can win each race, but the rest of us can feel like winners just for getting off our couches and into the streets where we belong. The general public who thinks skating is for kids is right. It is for the lost kid in all of us.

Skating brought back my own "lost kid." I traveled many emotional miles before getting to that Napa finish line, and beyond the self-limitations that I had built up over the years. From early childhood, it was my habit to put my life "on hold" until I was at "goal weight." It was extraordinarily important to my family that I be lean, and getting caught eating candy generated punishment for my own good.

My teens were spent refusing invitations using endless and urgent excuses, manufacturing reasons which increased in creativity to avoid swim parties. I claimed to suffer from numerous maladies from earaches to visiting relatives. My period was known to last five consecutive weekends, if necessary. The real excuse—"I am too fat"—was never uttered. I was waiting to be slim, and then life would start. Imprisoned by loneliness while other kids got together and had a ball was the penalty for being fat. My parents, sibling, television commercials and magazine covers with Twiggy on them told me I was fat. To me, being fat meant I deserved to suffer—and I did.

At five foot two and one hundred twenty-five pounds, I was grossly obese according to a *Cosmopolitan* magazine article. In those days, it was the periodical expert on all things female—be it beauty, femininity, how to put your best breast forward or how to catch and *keep* a man.

I went on a diet that lasted decades. I was either being "good" (hungry) or "bad," (eating too much cottage cheese and pineapple— or worse.) My character was defined by the contents of my plate and the scale on my bathroom floor—the "you're okay or you're not" meter.

For years, I watched the world through my bedroom window. I was "in hiding" when my weight was too high. *Other people* went to movies, rock concerts, out to dinner, on bike rides and on dates. They were at "normal" weight." I was not. As soon as I got slim, life would open up for me. My mother insisted people would like me then. The possibilities would be endless. Until then, I would wait in my room. Waiting to get small in an eleven-by-eleven-foot room took a long time. It took my whole youth. It took my whole spirit.

I knew I hurt my mother deeply because of my pounds. My weight was the only issue that separated us. I never asked her why she, the person who loved me the most, judged me so harshly on this one subject. I was often not allowed to eat the desserts the other family members would consume in front of me. Once when I was up ten pounds from a "successful" starvation diet that had me down to ninety pounds at age twenty, my mom referred to me in the past tense to my dad, saying, "Suzan used to be so pretty."

His response, "Yes, she was."

Standing in front of them, they spoke as if I were not present. I was full of shame for letting them down and not being the "best that I could be." I could not understand why I wanted food so badly when it hurt me in so many ways.

I was torn by guilt with every bite I took. I was pressed for time. "Hurry! Hurry! Get the weight off!" rang incessantly in my brain. While semifasting, it is hard to think of little else but food. The only real relief from the mounting pressure was to eat. I often caved in late at night. "Just this last one time. This *once*. I'll be good tomorrow." I promised this a hundred times to Jesus Christ, God, and myself. I meant it.

My youth passed along with the hope of weighing one hundred pounds. Time passed and I married Dennis Neary, a man who did not care if I was fat or thin. At least that is what he claimed. I gave him the chance to prove his sincerity when I gained seventy-five pounds during my first pregnancy. He held firm and true, though his gold, shaggy eyebrows twitched a bit when the nurse would announce my weight increase during each prenatal visit.

Years elapsed and I had another child, plus the three stepchildren I acquired when I married. Seven members of my own family died within eighteen months, including both of my parents and my grandmother, Gladyie. Somehow, along the way, I got lost in the passing of time and my spirit was put aside and forgotten. The mundane and tiring became routine. My essence was neglected. The demands of family and duty reigned over the nurturing of self. I was lost without going any place new.

Then came that day when Nancy strolled over and invited me to skate with her. I had felt devalued by giving up a job title, trading it in to be a full-time mom. I found answering cries a thousand percent more difficult than answering phones. Dennis' classic comment about my being tired from *only* watching children gave me the push I needed to escape from a cage I could not see, yet it thoroughly entwined me behind its invisible boundaries.

This act of defiance, coupled with feeling like a foolish adult and a bold youth all at the same time, started to create positive changes in my being. Similar upbeat changes occurred in my skating companions, too. As others joined me, I noticed a positive metamorphosis in woman after woman, man after man. A missing link in so many people is stirred up by the act of getting out in the fresh air and sometimes just getting fresh. Once the club got started, it became clear it was a fabulous way for all women, including larger ones, to exercise, have a laugh, and feel like a "Babe." This included women in their forties and fifties who were ready for something new. Many were starting life over after divorces or retirement.

The club opened up to male children when a "weekend dad," Frank Marsh, told me that his two little boys, seven- and nine-year-old Renny and Dustin, kept asking why they couldn't join when their eleven-year-old sister Nicholette, the club's only child member, got to be a Babe. By then, we had been in many newspapers and Nicole got to be in some pictures while they watched from the sidelines because they were boys. Frank said, "I just can't think of a way to explain to them why you won't let them in the club." Being left out because I was a girl was commonplace when I was growing up. If I had a buck for every time I heard "You can't because you are a girl," I could own a house in the Queen of England's neighborhood.

That is why, initially, I did not include men in the club. It was a bit of a stretch to call myself a Babe, and I did not think men qualified. I was wrong. Some men called me "sexist." That felt GREAT! I was a lobbyist when most people in politics were men and remembered being denied memberships to lobbyist clubs because I was female. It was payback time. I had reclaimed my Babe within and was living up to the Babe motto "It's my turn now." I thoroughly enjoyed the whining of those who wanted in but were not allowed because they were not female. I continued to relish the whining for several months until Frank came to see me about Renny and Dustin's wish to be in.

I pictured their faces, so cute and full of excitement about skating with the whole family. From that moment, the club was open to everyone. People of all shapes and sizes came forward. Uh, make that skated forward. Eighty men and boys joined this "women's" inline skating club in the next eight weeks. Heck, if men and boys want to wear a shirt that says "Babes on Blades" let them. They are the kind people I want to know. We call men "He-Babes" and children "Wee-Babes." I saw the self-esteem swell in person after person, and soon overweight children began to come and skate with their parents and their sense of confidence soared as well.

He-Babe Mark Richards, 38, when asked, "Why do you want to join a club called 'Babes on Blades?'" announced, "Where there are Babes, there is Mark." Babe Darlene assisted new skaters, especially larger women. The 200-plus-pound membership of the club grew to over fifty members the first year. The oldest member was 79, the youngest, two.

The club revitalized my soul. I had never had such a grand time and in such grand company, particularly as an overweight person. There I was rolling around in 1 and 2X—AKA large-sized clothing—and feeling sexy and sassy. My inner goddess was coming back to life. I skated mileage equal to the length and width of California—1400 miles—in honor of my mother who died of breast cancer. During those endless hours of skating, I promised the both of us that I would make a difference to at least sixty-five people I did not know. One for every year of my mother's life. Perhaps these would be people who thought the way Mom and I once did—that life does not begin until you are thin. I was on a mission to avenge this flawed thinking.

I quit my job and starting living off my savings or security blanket, risking most what made me feel safe. I abandoned my comfort zone to reach out to the public to lure them into trying something that could make them physically fit, feel better emotionally, and somehow release the spirit within that seeks expression—not repression—as mine had for so many decades.

Today, thanks to the Babes on Blades, I see others reclaim their own personal power, lost over the years for a long list of reasons, and miraculously found, right there along the asphalt. Each day holds new promise, as I observe women and men discover what I learned by participating in the Napa to Calistoga race—the biggest obstacle we have to face is our own old thinking. Throw on a pair of skates and in a short time, you too can feel so good, you will feel like a Babe.

Braking Technique practiced on California State University at Santa Barbara art form moments before campus patrol's arrival.

ADVENTURES IN INLINE SKATING

Ruminating from an alp top in Switzerland, clunking cowbells snap me out of a trance. I ponder how a summons to try something for the first time—inline skating—led to an avalanche of other "first times" at the age of forty-plus. From that first wobbly roll amid the sidesplitting laughter of rollers and witnesses alike, things changed forever. I got physically active and met people who experience the world in person, not just in their imaginations, enhanced by television and magazines. This seemingly juvenile undertaking was initially scary and then it got scarier as I found myself in front of large groups at sports shows—imagine me even attending one of those much less being a feature—and giving breakfast speeches for women's clubs. Press conferences about physical fitness 3,000 miles from home and regular television and radio appearances followed. This was not the life I ordered.

Other firsts included visiting unexplored cities and towns from a rolling, wind-in-your-face perspective. I wheeled through the sights, tastes and smells of San Francisco, Napa, Santa Barbara, Los

Angeles, Venice Beach, San Diego, Seattle, Portland, Indianapolis, Chicago, Amsterdam and Geneva—all on skates. This sport gave me a voice. That voice told my story—and the stories of many others—in syndicated newspaper and magazine columns. Here is a sampling of some of the works that used skating as a vehicle to promote self-esteem, self-acceptance and personal empowerment.

Give me a Brake

Ready to do it for the first time, we looked into each other's eyes—a blue pair and a green pair. Pupils enlarged with hope and anticipation mixed with fear and dread gave us slightly berserk expressions. Expelling simultaneous sighs, we realized the gravity of our decision and silently pondered the consequences. Gathering our courage and low-interest credit cards, Steph and I headed to the local sporting goods store. Our glazed eyes reflected our mission: purchasing inline skates. I was upgrading from the $39 pair that sat in the box for three years and Steph was moving up from her daughter's roller skates.

He lumbered at us with a smile, maneuvering around racks of heavy coats with fake fur collars and assorted skiwear.

"Hello, my name is Tim. What can I do for you fine ladies?" His blond crew cut had grown long enough to bend down in places. Tim looked as if he had been expecting us, the only customers in the small store. The place was packed from floor to ceiling with skiing, basketball, baseball, and backpacking equipment. Canoes and an inflated twelve-man raft rested against the far walls. Stephanie took it in with unblinking eyes.

Tim offered his expertise in selecting "Just the right skates for lovely ladies." "Don't worry," he soothed, "I am a professional skater."

He did not mention the dozens of manufacturers and styles of skates on the planet but gave strong attention and accolades to the skates mounted on the west wall—two brands, one model of each. One model. My eyebrows rose, probably crinkling my forehead, revealing my unspoken skepticism. To me, the "one model concept" is likened to a "one size fits all" bra.

Tim was very serious about getting Stephanie's toes, somewhat tender from a bout with corns caused by her high heeled sandals, into a pair of hard-shelled skate boots. He wrapped one of her feet in an oversized man's ski sock snatched from a basket near the cash register, and squeezed it, fat sock and all, into a skate he had selected off a wall mount. On one knee, he huffed. He puffed. And he pulled. He yanked the skate towards Steph, away from himself. A jiggle to the left, a wiggle to the right and Steph's ankle finally squeezed into place. Tim the sports salesman had a little trouble breathing as he yanked, with a grunt, the second skate onto Steph's other foot. He said it was a buckle problem, easily solved.

It was time to give me the same treatment. As he did, I silently studied the top of his head. He remained bent down on the other knee with perspiration glistening on his cheeks, which grew redder by the yank. I wondered if his glasses, encased in thick black frames, would slide down his nose and land on my foot. Steph and I exchanged clandestine glances. Putting on skates certainly took great effort.

At last, we were wearing the skates "designed with us in mind." Old enough to know better, we were suddenly transformed into adolescents encased in grown women's bodies. Stephanie squealed that she had not felt so free in years. We rolled around the store, laughing like four, instead of forty-year-olds. We hoped none of our neighbors would stroll by the shop and peek in the large windows.

"How do you stop?" asked Steph, her expression innocent but hopeful. She pushed her short white bangs out of her eyes as she spoke.

"Easy," the salesman answered, "just lift up your foot and put your heel down."

Sure enough, on the completely flat, smooth surface of the store carpet, it worked.

"Keep practicing," he encouraged sincerely. We purchased helmets and protective gear and headed home.

With renewed fervor and our buddy Nancy in tow, we strode onto our neighborhood street. Ignoring the hoots from the lawns of our neighbors, we approached a small hill with a gradual climb on one side and a steeper slope on the other. A mere pimple to an experienced skater, it was a summit to us. We were frightened but prepared. After all, we had learned from a professional skater.

"Heel up, toe down." Steph said it to herself out loud.

We climbed the gentler side of the hill and admired the view from its top. Along the steeper downhill was a row of houses with neat lawns and long driveways. At the bottom, the narrow road curved to the right, so the first skater would disappear from view of the other skaters. Knowing we would temporarily lose sight of each other, we aspired to meet at the end where the road intersects the highway. Primed and ready, we had a strategy: we would brake all the way down to control our speed, and celebrate our accomplishment at the bottom. We glided up, coasted over the tiny peak, and then collectively raised our right feet to engage the brake. We fell in unison - *plop, plop, PLOP*. The scraping of plastic safety equipment across pavement makes a ghastly sound. Pain can be forgotten, but it is impossible to forget a sound like that, once you have passed the age of thirty-five. For a few moments, our shock, mixed with surprise at being unbroken, was simultaneously frightening and exhilarating.

To the store

Frustrated but emboldened, Steph and I returned to the store. Our new safety equipment, bearing clear evidence that we had been to battle and prevailed, remained home. Instead of the "professional skater" from our previous visit, we were greeted by a rather tall, handsome young man, made taller by the skates he wore. They peeked out from under over-sized denim slacks that rested on top of his skate buckles. Born in the fifties, we overlooked his funny haircut but winced at the "earring" that poked out of his eyebrow. It looked like it should hurt. His name tag read *Nicholas*.

Stephanie took a deep breath and a big step forward. Looking directly into his nose hairs, she challenged, "Show me how to use the brake."

"You don't need the brake," said Nicholas to the top of her head. " It doesn't work. Take it off. When you want to stop, squeeze your legs—like snow plowing—and you'll stop. With some practice, it's easy."

A snowplow is a stopping technique where one points the toes inwards and the heels outwards, putting as much weight as possible over the latter to grind to a halt. We were not skiers, but after watching his demonstration, we tried his technique right there on the smooth, fluffy carpet. It worked very well.

On the hill

Fifty minutes later, we were back on the hill with Nancy in tow. I led the pack and snowplowed all the way down. Going only twice as fast as I wanted, I was energized by my accomplishment and felt renewed self-confidence welling up. Nancy's descent took a little longer—eleven minutes to be exact—because she artfully zigzagged back and forth, left to right, carefully proceeding inches at a time.

Then there was Steph. She contemplated her strategy atop the mountain until Nancy was ten minutes into her journey. Then, taking a deep breath, she made her move. She proceeded with caution. Within seconds, she realized that her legs would not form a snowplow the way they did on the store's even carpeting. She reached Nancy's ten-minute mark in forty-two seconds. The bearings in her wheels hummed as she zipped past gathering onlookers and flowerbeds. Hands and arms straight out in a Frankenstein's monster pose, with her legs wide apart, the forty-one-year-old mother of four reached the bottom of the hill still upright—a bit of a surprise to everyone. But she kept rolling. One neighbor, a blur to the left of Stephanie, cheered her bravery and balance. As Steph entered the straightaway, a sign for cross traffic came into view: **55 mph.**

With her body frozen in position and her wheels roaring under her, Steph flung her arms, still straight at the elbows, to the right and careened onto a narrow strip of grass. Still standing, she rolled six feet in high turf before her knees buckled and she lurched forward, falling perfectly flat, face down. It was like watching the ceremonial folding of a card table.

Our hearts lurched. Total silence reigned, interrupted only by cars whirling past on the road ahead. Suddenly, Steph lifted her head and peeked over the grass. Her neck was not broken; she was not lying face down in a shallow grave carved out in Paul and Gloria Schmidt's side yard. A roar of relieved laughter rose up from neighbors. From then on Steph was known as the "Banzai Babe"—a perfect handle for those that skate with no particular braking plan.

Making New Friends in Skating

I was excited about meeting my new friend in person. We had spoken over the phone several times. The subject was always about our love of skating and the things we had discovered about ourselves because of it. We agreed that our inline experiences gave us confidence and self-worth. We both had participated in the Napa to Calistoga event without meeting each other, and agreed we were better for the experience. We had proceeded despite our individual fears.

She was coming from another town to try the five-wheel "bumble bee skates" that Brian had given me. She wanted to test them before ordering a pair of her own, so Brian connected us. By then, I had skated in my pair at least a 100 times. Someone to skate with! My mind rushed. It would be a gas to have a skating buddy, a teammate. I would have company to join me as the caboose—the last person skating in large groups. We would attempt the 100 miler as a unit, I imaged with a big grin. My lack of speed did not diminish my love of skating with groups. I pictured us striding proudly with the back of the pack. I was so happy. I was so wrong.

She arrived and her long legs hoisted her high into the front door frame. She wore spandex pants, a bad sign. I had hoped for a frumpier exterior—an indicator of skill level. Or lack of skill level—an equal partner. She attached a brake that she had brought for the occasion, put the skates on, and was gone. Gone. She looked like an ice skater in inlines, as graceful as a swan parting calm waters instead of a skater rolling on the road. She said was afraid she would not be able to "cross over" because of the additional length of skate. Crossover. That was a new one. I thought that was something you did to railroad tracks or something the Norwegians do to waffles. No, there she and her long legs were, stepping skate over skate over skate, traveling smoothly forward. I tried it and met the neighbors grass, blade to blade. My six stabs at the pavement in my four-wheeled skates were matched by her one long continuous glide.

We came up over the hill that Steph, Nancy and I had attempted to learn to brake on. She put her toes up, heel down and stopped. Just like that. I had never seen such a thing. I had no brake. The guy at the store told me they did not work and took mine off and threw it away. I used God and loud, sincere prayers as my brake. God, the snowplow, and fear stopped me. And sometimes fear did not work so good, and neither did the snowplow, especially on steep grades. This woman, my new companion, put her foot up and stopped again. Her neck was not thrown forward. Her body remained perfectly erect. I tried to study her technique but sailed by—unable to stop!

The 100-mile event that took on the hills of San Francisco was in six days. I would be wearing my five-wheeled, currently brakeless skates. She looked at my skate, she looked at me, and then she looked at my skate. She squinted and moved in close, looking directly into my sunglasses.

"You'd better get a brake and learn how to use it before next weekend."

Boy, without a doubt something told me she knew *exactly* what she was talking about.

"Cheer up," I told myself, "you have a whole week to get a brake and learn how to stop." The day before the race, I still could not stop using solid will and skill. I had to give in to the thought this would be another *fear-based* skate. But I was going. I had skated long enough to know if I crawled up a hill or down, it was no particular reflection on my worthiness as a person. So I went.

The wisdom of my new friend's words revealed itself time and again as I sailed down streets as high as mountain tops, arms outstretched, legs wide in a snowplow/splits combo, lips pulled back revealing a ghastly grin of terror. It wasn't pretty, but I skated my age in miles, and then Dennis drove me the other 60 just in time to see the winner of the race, thirty-year-old Dan Burger, cross the finish line. He was clean cut, neat and "*sweeeeeeeeeeet.*" Studying him carefully, I again thanked God for putting me in skates.

By the way, my new skating buddy did all 100 miles, but I got a better look at the winner.

Insatiable

One night I strapped a ten-pound weight belt around my middle. Its function is to maximize workouts. Then—with confidence, zeal and daring—I zipped up and down the two mile street in front of my suburban home. My wheels assaulted the road for fifteen miles. After that, I took the belt off and did seven miles more. I was animal-like. My neighbors watched me from their kitchen windows. I was high! The endorphins were roaring and so was I. The grin spread across my face made me look possessed. I saw this with my own eyes in the refection off Al Jellum's 1964 Ford pickup truck window. I was happy! I skated behind innocent neighbors walking their dogs then whipped around them just in time. Obnoxious teenager? No! An exuberant over-forty-year-old punk! From mouse to monster, that was me. Sometimes I would go backwards and do a few circles. I was hot and I knew it! So hot I knew if I touched myself, my finger would ignite. *Hisssssssss.*

Workmen were replacing the roofs on three homes along the route. You know what they say about those tacky contractors and their chauvinistic ways of shouting at women. These boys did not have the chance. I hooted and I hooted first. I was too fast to hear their responses. Except once. I heard one say, "I'd sure like to...." His words trailed off. Too much speed. Risking it all I retorted, "Go ahead, but you'll have to catch me *first.*"

Whoa! I was feeling my oats, all right! I was full of them. Imagine *me* of all people—a woman with babies and a husband waiting at home. The woman who wore the same oversized shorts for five summers in a row. I hid inside them. Then, I put on inline skates and, baby, something hidden deep inside me came out. It was all I could do to get out of my own way.

Out of control and loving it. I was confident. More confident than ever before. I didn't want to stop. But it got dark.

Later, Fabulous Fred Festerson, our neighbor, came over. He had seen my show of speed, strength, and daring. He could not believe his eyes. He admired the new muscles in my legs. Every part of me felt marvelous. Even the cellulite seemed to lose its negative pull on my spirit. I was possessed.

The phone rang. Fred grabbed it and blurted out, "Stay away from here! There's something wild about Suzan! She's *insatiable!*"

What a word! And it was used to describe *me.* Yesterday's "You look like you could use a vacation" is today's "*insatiable!*" Imagine that! Give me a little skate time and I become *insatiable. Roooooaaar!*

Roll-Away Skates

It had been two months since I had done it. I wondered if it would feel the same. Would there be the same bombardment of emotions the second time? Round #2 of the Napa to Calistoga Skate Race in Northern California was soon to commence. I envisioned the twenty-seven-mile route and its lavish vineyards that looked like green blankets thrown over the hillside. Scenery aside, I most clearly remembered the hill and my spill. The double yellow line in the middle of a road looks very different when you lie *on top* of it.

Having only a few months experience under my wheels the first time I approached the "Roll Through the Wine Country," I had been a little hesitant. Actually, it was more like the most frightening thing I had *forced* myself to do in my adulthood. I had packed up my anxieties and shown up. The result changed me beyond my most positive expectations. I fin-ished the race. It was not a com-petition between other skaters and me. It was one between me and the bondage of self. It was a new and unexpected begin-ning of positive things to come.

At last, it was time to begin again! Colorfully appareled racers lined up and took off. The pros left first, the citizen class last. And that is close to where I finished, almost last. But that did not matter. I felt victorious because I was there.

The road was smoother than I remembered. Monstrous hills had mysteriously flat-tened out. I had fallen on a downhill the first time because I was trying to reduce speed.

Babes shared their antics on television to lure the innocent public to join them.

31

My fear of falling caused me to fall. This time I stopped trying to control everything and went with the flow. I screamed with glee all the way down. Exhilarating! I had actually improved from the first race!

I finished eighty-first out of eighty-six skaters. I gloriously passed a couple from Long Beach, California, on the last down hill. Dennis observed this feat from the opposite side of the road. His arms waved high in the air as he loudly cheered, "You *actually* passed somebody!"

I also beat an eight-year-old boy and his forty-five-year-old mother. Ah, it was good to be back at Napa to reclaim the winner hidden deep inside.

Skating in the City by the Bay

It was a true excursion—exceptional. What made it exceptional? Surely, the distance of one hundred miles from my doorstep is not that far. The location—San Francisco—heck, even my relatives from Indiana have been *there*.

It was special because *I* made the trip, escaping the internal ball and chain that ties me to an unforgiving sense of daily duty, clutching my spirit daily. It is that invisible shoulder-tapper that pokes me awake every morning reminding me there is much to be done. Half of that lurks from the *To Do* list of yesterday and *Who-Knows-What* list of today. That usually takes up thirty lines of paper, leaving plenty of room for the unpredictable.

"Let's take a day off and go to the city," my gal pal Sal said, during a business meeting.

My head seemed to spin around twice before it stopped to process the information.

"Take a day off? I silently repeated to myself. Must be hallucinating. How unfair. I was too young to take drugs in the sixties and there I was suffering from hallucinations like I had when Brian suggested I do Napa.

When one workaholic says to another, "Let's take a day off" there has to be a chemical imbalance or synapse dysfunction somewhere. My pal is one of those people who reeks confidence and can get right to the heart of the matter requiring few words to manipulate her subject.

"There are lots of places to skate there."

No need to argue. She had won.

Golden Gate Park. It had been twenty years, 100,000 loads of laundry, 200 packs of disposable power diapers, and 500 excuses since my last visit. Craning my neck to see the tops of three hundred-foot-high trees with trunks the width of small car, I pinched myself. We had traveled light years away from the little town of Loomis where I live. I stood in a place so different from where I had come, not far in geographical miles, but separated by about one million in my mind. No matter how good something sounds, if it is more than one excuse or twelve ounces of energy away, I do not consider it when caged inside another busy day.

People meandered everywhere. "What are they doing out in the fresh air on a weekday?" I wondered. Cars, skaters, walkers, joggers, bikers, birds chirping, the smell of eucalyptus—does all this go on every day without me?

I sought out a paved path that circled the park. You could not miss the message painted on it: "*NO SKATING.*" Not the welcome a skater longs for.

I cinched on my helmet and carefully glided forward into the street. I was in the Big City on skates! Suddenly, this concerned me. There are hills in this city. In lieu of speed bumps, they have paved mountains dotted with cars. I tucked my concerns inside my fanny pack and rolled.

My pal passed me on her bike. I tried to stay out of the way of the cars coming up from behind, thus putting myself in line of the bumpers of parked cars in front. I finally figured out what other folks did. They used the road as if they owned it.

"There's a car behind you!" I shouted to my friend.

"Let 'em go around me," she casually shot back from her bike.

I was shocked! I did not want skaters to get the reputation of being road hogs. Single-mindedly, I decided to set a good example for all, completely forgetting I was forbidden to use the off-traffic trail evidenced by the *NO SKATING* sign. I was traveling in the street—the last available option to me except for staying home—at which I excel. I made it my personal duty to uphold a higher standard and inconvenience no motorist. Onward I wheeled.

This time the parked car I almost smacked was a Lexus. It was so clean I probably would have slid over the top and down the windshield in one smooth motion before plopping onto concrete. I suddenly understood mainstream mentality and enjoyed the wisdom of it, and skated in the street like I owned it.

Skating through the park was like visiting heaven for a day— buffalo hung out to my right, gargantuan trees reached to the sky on my left, and fluffy clouds floated above. Wind whipped over my helmet, bringing the smell of freshly cut grass with it. My blood pumped like crazy and my weighty concerns of only three hours earlier melted away magically.

My friend shouted, "Makes your problems seem small," as she whizzed past. Clearly, she was on to something. Getting out of my mental clutter was the best vacation I had in ages, and I didn't know it only took saying "yes" to an unexpected invitation to do something that seemed *unproductive.*

We came to the end of the journey—Highway 101. It is that stretch of roadway that travels along the pounding Pacific Coast. Standing there in my skates, I took in the view of the waves. In my mind the adventure was fabulous, but over. Luckily feet, having no brains, do not think. For some reason, mine took off up HWY 101.

Wondering what I would find each minute, my skates hammered the pavement, scooting around sand and occasional driftwood. Cars passed and I pressed forward. For two hours I skated my heart out with my friend close behind acting as car watch dog and safety announcer.

When it was over I was exhausted, wet, and completely alive. A light that had been buried deep under the darkness of doubt shined up through me. For the first time, I understood something about the self-propelled people you pass in your car every day.

Again, my skates took me on a voyage I have not seen promised in tour books. It was one of unanticipated physical and mental exhilaration. They rolled me far away from my reasonable, thinking mind, to a place minds cannot manufacture. They took me out of myself, and the ride was glorious.

The Friday Night Skate

It clung to the dented bumper on a ragged, primer gray VW bus. "There's no gravity, the earth sucks." The auburn-topped hair-to-waist chap with his sports-bra-bearing, Hanes-underwear-wearing female counterpart vigorously embraced those words as they danced on their inline skates twirling tip toe over tip toe over whoa! There was no gravity that Friday night in San Francisco, at least not in the parking lot of the Embarcadero's Ferry Building where this skater and hundreds of others gathered and played for an hour or so before our 8:30 p.m. departure into the lighted bowels of the city.

Your life, not to mention the lives of hundreds of others, will pass before and all around you when you slip on your skates and join the "The Midnight Rollers."

Bodies absorb into a dazzling mass of man/womankind at its most colorful—and unpredictable—at least fashionwise. Lawyers, bankers, tie-dyed hippie wannabes, and those in-between become a mobile adventure tour. Time to see a famous city in a brand-new way.

Donning a silver, rhinestone turban anchored to his forehead by a multi-colored, blinking headband, the leader of the pack, the ever-smiling, forty-something He-Babe David Miles cranked up the music from his white van. It held a stereo system and speakers the size of some of the skaters. Miles did a pirouette of his own and his red-wheeled skates became a blur, as did the rest of him, turban, lights and all. Known as the Godfather of Skating, tonight's attire could qualify him as "The Liberace of Skating." The speed of his spin intensified just like energy of the crowd. There was something and someone for everyone. We were getting high on the breezy air and just being there and the first-time visitors were ready to roll who-knows-where.

The history of the skate started innocently enough. After the 1989 Loma Prieta earthquake, the double-decked Embarcadero Freeway was closed to traffic. Its miles of smooth, car-free asphalt proved irresistible to skaters who began to meet there regularly. The freeway was eventually torn down but the seed was planted. What started with eight skaters grew to 500 "regulars" with occasional highs of 700 participants.

At the appointed departure time, David paused before the crowd, "Don't do anything to make the cops mad. Remember they can give you a ticket for running red lights so be cool!" He introduced a team from the Outdoor Channel doing a special on the group. Miles welcomed first-time skaters and reminded the crowd that flashing florescent tubes of light perfect for necks, helmets or *whatever* were for sale for five bucks. With that, the crowd commenced to thump-thump-thump over the initial route of wooden planks along the waterfront. A quarter of a mile ahead was a forty-eight-year-old Mountain View man, perched atop a statue of an anchor along the pier. He sported a protective pair of skate shorts whose manufacturer promises will help you "say goodbye to road rash, bruises and busted butts" by offering thick foam pads sewn right into the shorts (in strategic places.) He was among the faster skaters waiting for the slower ones to catch up as he nestled there on his foam.

At different points in the route, a "counter" shouted numbers to skaters as they passed, letting them know where they fell in the line up. Beverly Christensen of American Parkway Drive in Sacramento once found herself in position 195, and another time 505, "too busy gawking perhaps." There were 703 in all that night.

Another product proudly displayed by some was "Punky Color," a semi-permanent hair dye that comes in bright red, pink, orange, blue, purple, and green. The packaging promises that it is "great for getting elderly folks to stare." When encountering "Punky Color" hairdos, even some teenagers stared with the best of the old fogies. When a blaze of rainbow Lycra topped by florescent purple zooms past, it can be hard not to stare and even harder not to point it out to a friend, or even a complete stranger with a "Did you get a load of *that?*" It is a relatively safe question if the person you pose it to appears to be more normal than he probably is. Many skaters that night were not above pointing. Perhaps they felt they would not get caught in all the commotion.

Up the hill lime green glowworm necklaces from blocks ahead wiggled around necks perched on all sizes and dimensions of bodies, some miraculously sealed in spandex. The lime wove among blinking hills of humanity that swirled around, ahead and behind each other. One could see them as far as five and six stop lights away, a mile ahead up the hillside.

Culture lovers experienced the Palace of Fine Arts from a new viewpoint. Beneath the massive palace dome, skaters joined hands and whipped each other around in a frenzy that frightened the meek. A giant of a man clutched the frail wrist of a skinny woman dressed in an itsy-bitsy red skirt, of all things, and propelled her into the fray. Some of the screams under that dome could have been hers, or dozens of others who seemed to take great delight in being swallowed in swirling helmeted humans. The people on the outside of the fray whipped faster than those holding center positions. Faster and faster they spun, providing an opportunity to see one's own life pass before her eyes—in more ways than one.

Over the thirteen-mile course, skaters would hoot at cars that honked in response. This set in motion a succession of more hooting and more honking. This sound resonated in deafening proportions in tunnels. We traveled down a narrow steel sidewalk paralleling the pavement in one tunnel. The vibrations created a thunderous echo that bounced off the ceiling of the medal structure. Seven hundred pairs of skates—each with four or five wheels—created a roar that I could feel in my internal organs. A visitor from Hong Kong called it, "Big noise leaving no room for other sound."

One two-mile tunnel of honking cars, howling skaters, and clanking skate wheels reverberated within the massive tube with such an electrifying energy that many of the skaters simply could not stop vibrating after exiting the tunnel. Their shouts and hollers at full lungs out continued as they passed restaurants and innocent shoe-clad pedestrians. This was the place to be, according to forty-nine-year-old Gail Brown raised by life-long Republicans in a town called Loomis that boasts 8,250 residents. Same planet, different world.

Martha Ketcher, hailing from San Pedro said, "What really impresses me is that instead of going to bars and drinking the stress of a long work week away, they are skating past the bars." Well, most did.

They took a break at an intersection with shops all around. Skaters, friendly and high on the moment, enthusiastically returned any single greeting offered by pedestrian or passenger, with seven hundred "Yos," hoots and various spirited utterances having no proper spelling in English.

"I am proud to be a part of this colorful gang of hippies, professional people, athletes, nonathletes, first-time skaters, can you imagine, teeny boppers, moms, dads, and even people in their sixties and seventies," claimed Mario Ricchi of Vallejo. It was his first time though, "I've wanted to do this for two years. Tons of my friends come up here to do it and now I know why."

"Sometimes when there is a whole lot of people, it gets crazy," someone casually understated.

Along the route glided "Screaming Barney," named for the purple Barney character strapped to a well-lit helmet that cast beams of light in four directions. This skater from Vallejo set a good example by not running the red light like those before him. Barney, twenty-sevenish explained, "It's better to be behind the line than under a car."

David Clark, a forty-three year old chemist from Alameda, gracefully maneuvered his thirtieth curb of the evening behind a jogging stroller containing his three-year-old daughter Olive, who was properly belted and helmeted for the occasion. His ten-year-old son Graham followed, somehow not losing sight of them in the sea of moving humanity.

After three hours, the adventure was over. Long after its completion, our spirits remained skyward. Some went dancing to burn off the adrenaline and others continued skating in a dark world illuminated by their experience and the lights of San Francisco. Others headed home, anxious for the week to pass so they could do it all over again.

Dennis Lapchis, founder of the Washington Inline Skating Association, drove out from Seattle for the experience. Lapchis was used to skating in large groups. A week later he said, "I was blown away to see entire streets taken over by skaters with the cooperation of motorists and the police. I could not believe my eyes! I couldn't believe I was a part of it! I was high for three days afterwards!" This left him only four days until the next Friday Night Skate, where for three hours you can leave your shoes, and the real world, far, far behind.

Skate Clubs are Fun!

3

Skating Clubs

Skating clubs attract the unpredictable. You'll see. Clubs pull in different kinds of people with a multitude of interests and talents who offer fresh ideas for fun things to do on skates. The companionship is uplifting. All over the globe, skate clubs participate in a variety of events from simple weekly get-togethers to massive special events. The sport is a great equalizer as doctors and lawyers glide with tattoo artists and receptionists with bright blue hair. Your skates enable you to see nearby neighborhoods whose details you may have missed when you zoomed past in the car. Clubs sometimes take us beyond our borders into new cities and lands.

When traveling to a new city, take your skate bag. Look up skate clubs in the area by doing a search on the Internet or ask local skate retailers once you get there. If you have time beforehand, research will pay off and you may be able to speak with the club president or group skate leader over the phone or via e-mail and arrange to skate with local residents.

Check out http://www.skating.com/ or www.iisa.org to find clubs. These sites will also provide numerous links on a variety of inline skating topics.

In this section, you will find a series of adventures that the Babes on Blades enjoyed as a club. These articles appeared in the syndicated Babes on Blades newspaper sports column. This is a small example of the fun you can have as a Babe *and* in a club.

Babes on Parade

When was the last time you played in the middle of the road? Babes on Blades did just that by throwing themselves passionately into the streets of Roseville, USA, when they took on the Annual Chamber of Commerce Christmas Parade.

Understanding "best is often saved for last," the Babes were number 296 in the line up of parade participants. Restless Babes glided back and forth, awaiting the call: the call of the wild. Finally, they were off! In, out and all about, Babes, swiveled around convertibles bearing beauty queens, float-loaded flatbeds, dozens of '55 Chevys, bicycles, tractors, men, women, children, and beasts. The dotted yellow line in the road served as a stimulus as some Babes practiced technique, weaving between the gold markings. Bright orange cones became part of a makeshift obstacle course until the Babes realized humans were more fun *and* challenging because sometimes they move. High school marching bands played wonderful tunes accompanied by lads and ladies holding giant letters spelling out the names of their schools. I made a daring dash between the double "L" in "Roseville" for which I was applauded by the crowd and scolded by an unknown stick-in-the-mud. For the most part, the Babes stayed out of trouble, though that was not their intention. They did set good examples, however, by wearing helmets and safety gear, waving to the crowd, saying please and thank you and giving candy to children and the elderly.

It was exhilarating to skate through the town's center, bursting with thousands of people on the sidelines. The air was thick with excitement, anticipation, and the smell of horses prancing ahead. Old Town looked very different from the center lane. I felt like a child, not knowing what the next moment would bring and somehow expecting a "real adult" to tell us to go home. No harsh words or glares under contorted eyebrows came at us. Instead, "Babes on Blades!" burst forth from sidewalk witnesses. I looked at my skates: nine months ago I did not know what inline skates were. Now I was in the company of thirty "Babes," most of whom had only recently discovered skating. We glided, somewhat wobbly at times, filled with an adventure not dreamed past the age of seven. Skating in a parade in downtown, USA—what could be next for the Babes?

Leading the hubbub was Babe Andy who traveled on his unicycle, clearing the path for the Babes when horses left obstacles on the course. Smack in front of the judges as the Babes were introduced to the public, Andy made a smooth dismount with plastic pooper-scooper in hand. A generous plop of road apples was captured in a single swoosh—the scrapping of plastic against asphalt added to the wonderful sounds of the day. Andy's unique contribution was announced over the loud speaker. How he deposited the offending prize is unknown, but I noticed he ignored my shouts of "Throw it into the crowd, Andy!"

A woman appeared at the end of our route and presented Babe Kathleen with a bouquet of flowers. "I have never seen my forty-eight-year-old child on skates, much less in a parade on skates," she said.

Meeting new people, seeing new sights, and extending your "childhood" into your 30s, 40s, 50s and beyond, is what skating is all about. I dare you to try it.

The Babes Abandon the Streets for the Rink

In their never-ending quest for fun, exercise and flirtation with danger, the Babes on Blades inline skating club escaped from the streets where they normally play and did the unexpected—they headed indoors.

Babes on Blades membership has grown somewhat out of control, like weeds in a garden. These Babes rarely skate under roofed structures because they are invigorated by fresh air. Indoor occasions typically become short-lived ventures. Numbers of Babes, in search of a quick refreshment or sandwich, have been just as quickly rolled out of grocery stores by the management.

This was not the case recently when fifty-seven Babes abandoned bumpy roads for the perfectly smooth maple floors of a roller rink. The management not only greeted the Babes with open wrist guards, but the owner, Michael Jacques, donned a "He-Babe!" shirt. The Babes took on the rink, the snack bar, and the general public with their usual zest, enthusiasm and colorful shirts.

"I really enjoyed myself," said Lonnie Albright of Folsom. When asked her age, Lonnie answered, "Fifty-four 'til April and then it gets worse." In commenting about her experience she said, "At first I was intimidated when I saw all the kids swirling around then I got enthused about skating with the Babes."

Another member, who asked not to be identified because she called in sick to her employer to make the two-hour drive to join the Babes, said, "I didn't know anybody, but I have wanted to skate at night for a long time. As soon as I walked in wearing the Babe T-shirt, it was as if I had fifty automatic friends. I'll be back for more," she promised, "at least until my boss finds out."

Some Babes glided with arms out-stretched, legs wide open and mouths agape as they ambled forward with a degree of uncertainty. They exposed the indoor crowd to a new style of travel ranging from "I'm a Babe and proud of it" to "I hope no one saw what I just did."

It took little time for some Babes to gain new confidence as they took on the indoor challenge. Gary Mohler, 43, of North Highlands, said, "Due to the smoothness and lack of obstacles, it encouraged me to try new things. I felt comfortable practicing moves I had not tried before." Shortly after, He-Babe Gary seemed quite willing to live up to his quote as he posed probing questions regarding the after-skate plans of a lovely "She-Babe" gliding past.

Babes traded the threat of smacking the asphalt, which can be unforgiving, for a new surface that rewarded their tumbles with a gentle slide-a-while glide immediately followed by a return-to-your-feet-and-keep-rolling maneuver, all with one smooth continuous motion.

Some Babes were quick to note that children, some no more than three feet tall, were fearless on skates, weaving in, out and all about effortlessly like a bee buzzing over a flower bed. Babes endured such stampedes and miraculously, no hit-and-run rolls were reported.

Many club members were happy to trade curbs, car horns and water bottles for a flat surface, music with a beat, and a Slurpy. One participant saw skating with more than 200 people as an opportunity to hone quick decision-making skills such as: "Should I try to stop, clobber the six-year-old on my right or the sixty-year-old on the left?" in response to another skater's unanticipated stop straight ahead. In the seconds it took to consider a choice, the options had skated away. Suddenly he was hot on the trail of a couple facing him — gliding backwards. Confused, he thought *he* had somehow maneuvered himself in the wrong direction and corrected himself so *he* was skating backwards only to view 100 people coming his way. What happened after that is unclear but he purchased a Babes on Blades membership as a gift for a friend whom he claimed deserved a change of pace.

Babes birthday bash with Brian Snelson, K2 rep

Ronda Gates, 55, of Portland, Ore, typically an outdoor skater, viewed the rink philosophically. "Each trip around is a metaphor for the circle of completion I strive for in my own life. My resolution this year," she said, "is to start less and finish more. This gave me an opportunity to get in the rhythm of that."

"Wee-Babe" Adam Richards, 4, of Roseville, had a different perspective. "The best part were the games," he said. "I had fun, but my dad wouldn't buy me candy."

The daring Gerri Adams, 44, of Cortland, practiced doing the forward splits. Her efforts landed her a seat on the maple. "I'll be back to slide, I mean try, again," she promised.

If you are an outdoor skater and want to take a stab at indoor skating, call a rink in your area. Inquire about their inline skating policies and programs. Ask if you can bring your own skates. If your skate bolts are flush with the frame, chances are you can. Bolts that stick out can scratch the floor's surface, and are not allowed. A new bolt often provides a simple solution. Some rinks rent inline skates, which is a handy way to introduce a hesitant friend to the sport. They get the thrills of rolling without the consequences of falling on cement. Many rinks have special times for adult-only skates, family skates packages, plus lessons. If you are ready to trade the great outdoors for an indoor adventure, I highly recommend you gather your skates, a few friends, and discover what awaits you under an air-conditioned roof.

Babes Jumped and Shot All Day

Excellent California He-Babe Terry Dent invited the Babes to be a part of a promotional film his company was producing to extol the proficiency of its highly sophisticated equipment. He worked for Tektronix Grass Valley Products, manufacturer of professional broadcasting and video products. Here is the resulting commotion.

Getting jumped. There is something negative about that phrase. Broadcasters do not say it with a smiling face on the evening news. That is because the "jumper" or the "jumpee" is not a Babe. *I am a Babe.*

Babes had a splendid time getting jumped recently in a local community park by a He-Babe, as thirty-five fellow Babes hooted, cheered and waited their turn. The sun was shining and life was good on that Saturday morning as my buns nestled on the warm cement awaiting the next lunge.

Stunt skater and master of defying gravity, the high hopping Matt LaCross, celebrity athlete, skate model, skate designer, and most important of all—He-Babe—flew out from Seattle all the way to Roseville, California to join the Babes on Blades. Despite a little apprehension, I casually invited Matt to jump me while we waited for the cameras to get rolling, acting as if it were a request I made every day.

Picture yourself when *you* grow up. See yourself lying on your back, on concrete, in a public park at mid-day with some 26-year-old wonder boy jumping over you as you squint into the sun? Con-

sider that the shadow cast over your face for an instant is from four tiny wheels that can leave skid marks on asphalt. Let us not think about what they would leave on your face if they touched down.

I never aspired for such a moment in my reckless youth. Now, as a "grown-up", that is exactly what I was doing. I lay down and waited, breathlessly at times, screaming at others, to see what would happen as a talented athlete did magnificent tricks in the air, with me underneath. I prayed out loud for his success. His record, feats, and talent are without question. So is the fact that I am a chicken. I was overshadowed by the relentless power of my fear-based personality and practical reasoning mind, which chanted, "He's only human." If he miscalculates a landing or had a muscle spasm, will I survive the embarrassment, or die instantly? Never mind. I leaned back and discovered, as LaCross dashed at me, I found it to my liking. After a few overhead hops, I heard a voice. It was mine. It said one word: "More."

Other Babe members got into the fray and joined me on the ground. LaCross kept coming, and we just kept begging for more, our numbers were growing on the path and his hurls became higher, longer and wider to accommodate our expanding horizontal posturing. Picture a dozen or so "adults" in their thirties, forties and up, who a few months earlier were afraid to even try the sport of inline skating, suddenly arguing over who gets jumped next.

They were more than willing to throw themselves into a good cause, though Babes made no effort to behave themselves between and during takes. The film will be shown at the National Association of Broadcasters' convention in Las Vegas to champion the expertise of Tektronix as a top manufacturer in its field. The antics of the Babes will be viewed by over 100,000 broadcasters and who-knows-what will happen from there.

Babes, lively moving targets, were shot from all directions as they frolicked freely before the cameras pointed right at them. Shy at first, some Babes resisted being filmed, but got over it.

The filming started in Roseville and moved to the paved trail along the American River. The scenery was spectacular and so was the human element. Perhaps inspired by the sight and sounds of nature, the Babes got frisky at the second location. At times eight or more would get into the act and plop on the pavement in a colorful clump, beckoning LaCross to dash up and over them while skating down a steep hill. He never missed his mark, lucky for the helmets below and the forty-thousand-dollar movie camera beyond, which he leapt over, too.

Matt LaCross and I had done television programs before, with Matt jumping and spinning over chairs, stairs, rails, furniture and occasionally this Babe, if he could catch me. I do not skate very fast, sometimes on purpose.

Inline skating continues to provide the unpredictable, to put it mildly. It is the perfect sport for four-year-olds, tykes in their sixties, and everyone else in between. If you have not given it a whirl, or in some cases a whirl-twirl-swirl, I dare you to try it. Who knows, along the way you may get jumped and shot in the best sense of the words—and come out feeling like a Babe.

Babes Boogie in the Big Apple

Who ever said, "Life begins after forty" is right. I stand behind that statement with my whole heart, and the rest of my body, for two reasons—the first is obvious—it is correct—the second is more obvious—I am over forty. That year crept up on me like a cat sneaking up on a fat finch poking for worms in the back yard—very slow but very sure. I was not looking when forty nabbed me, and I have not looked back since. Suddenly, I was not alone. I was a part of a group, a team, a *big* team. People over forty are not shy—they demand to be heard and they are everywhere. This is comforting in my old age. Ha ha, don't throw rocks.

The world is changing and sometimes I do not like it. But what I do like is being seen as important, even if it is by manufacturers who want my money. It used to be that those selling almost *everything* targeted youth. This was great when I was a youth, and my mother was paying the bills, but after that, it lost its charm. Now retailers, particularly those in the fitness and sports industries, are realizing yesterday's youths are today's forty-and-over set. And these folks are redefining old. They do not retire at fifty; they take up inline skating and karate and other sports. Some have kids in elementary school. They are active and ageless and the sporting goods manufacturers recognize this—at long last.

The Sporting Goods Manufacturers Association (SGMA) is the

The Big Apple Loves Babes, as does Al Roker

North American trade association of more than 2,000 manufacturers and national brand distributors of sports apparel, athletic footwear, fitness and sporting goods equipment. Founded in 1906, the SGMA's primary mission is to promote sports, recreation and fitness, and to foster market growth and vitality. They put out an *Active and Ageless Resource Guide* created to help men and women, ages fifty-plus, locate groups in their areas that enjoy physical activity, be it dancing, aerobics, inline skating, bowling, billiards and more.

The SGMA co-sponsored an event in late 1999 with the United Nations celebrating the "International Year of the Older Persons." In this case "older" is over fifty—like it or not. It saluted the seventy-two million Americans who are living longer, fuller and healthier lives than ever before, in a two-day extravaganza that took place in New York City plus 400 cities around the world. SGMA flew out three Babes on Blades—Pat Musselman, 68, of Citrus Heights, Sandy Adsit, 59, of Rocklin, and this youngster at 44, to assault the asphalt in the Big Apple and serve and swerve as role/roll models or "examples" during the festivities.

The Babes appeared in full gear in a Manhattan fashion show, plus in the United Nations building, on radio and television, including an outside appearance on The Today Show, and local appearances chasing each other and sometimes the crowd. They parted pigeons and pedestrians in Central Park and maneuvered around yellow cabs on Seventh Avenue for Hispanic television until authorities put a stop the ruckus and made us come indoors before a

49

cab nailed us. Members of the growing crowd booed.

US News and World Report featured Sandy and Pat noting that sporting goods retailers need to refocus from mostly targeting the youth market and recognize the ever-increasing numbers of baby boomers and those older. According to the article, the sporting goods manufacturers are "better known for catering to the hip-hop and bubble-gum set, (but) the industry has discovered that the fastest-growing segment of its market is ripe for membership in the AARP." It went on to state that those 45 and older accounted for sports apparel sales of $8.6 billion dollars in 1999—up $1 billion over the previous year. The numbers are rising fast for sales of exercise equipment and gym memberships, too. The dilemma for the industry is breaking out of youth-only oriented marketing. Still, the author of the *US News and World Report* story initially could not believe anyone over fifty would *dare* inline skate.

"Impossible!" she insisted. "You mean to tell me you encourage people *that age* to put on rollerblades?" I assured her that in the past three years I had taught inline skating to over 1500 people who are fifty and over. It was usually their first time on skates but not the last. Not bad for a generation that had few mentors over forty when it came to exercise. Their fitness icons were mostly Olympic champions and multi-million dollar athletes who possessed bodies very different from their own.

If you are under forty—you have much to look forward to—in part because the role models *you* have demonstrate that you can be active all your life. If you are over forty, you are probably too busy reclaiming *your* Babe within to sit down long enough to read this article.

See you out there.

We assumed this sign meant skaters, too.

On right, first Babes on Blades chapter president Reed Warner, Seattle, Washington, with K2 public relations guru Matt LaCross and Suzan Davis. Men sneered and women cheered upon hearing "Babes chose Reed as the Seattle Babe president because he has qualities that Babes admire – youth and good looks." Below, Babes at play.

Babes on Blades inline skating across Holland

4

Skate Travels

Tripping Out on Skates

Inline skating drew me not only out of my neighborhood, but also out of myself. This embellished my spirit mightily. One's inner spirit is like the front yard, you can mow it on Friday, but if you do not maintain it, it becomes choked with weeds in a short time. When I do not get out of my small, busy world, I cannot get out of the relentless chatter in my head. This getting out is not easy to do between caring for children, work, and other responsibilities that befall Babes, but you reap great rewards when it happens.

Babes Away, Skating in Anchorage, Alaska

Waiting for a shuttle at Anchorage airport, I wonder what the long, narrow cases lined up in a neat row along the curb contain. I am not the only one wondering.

"What in the world do you have in a bag shaped like *that*?" he asks, nodding towards my skate-shaped tote. Startled from my private thoughts, I look into a handsome, weatherworn face. The flannel wearing, fur hat-bearing male is baffled.

"Inline skates," I boast. "Going to burn some calories here in Alaska while seeing the sights." With squinting eyes, I attempt to hide my uncertainty about finding a place to skate in the vast wilderness of Alaska.

"How 'bout you?" I look toward one of the long, steel cases.

"Huntin' season. Rifle here, bullets there, good-bye grizzly bear." A wide smile of anticipation emphasizes deep lines in his face. His sentence lingers and his eyebrows rise over sparkling green eyes. I realize he is not sweating under all those warm clothes; he is leaking testosterone.

What do you picture when you think of Alaska? Massive glaciers? Sparkling blue ice layered with igloos? Eskimos with their dogs pulling sleds? How about snow-covered peaks prowled by polar bears hunting for seals and salmon or moose and large fuzzy wolves dwarfed by larger and fuzzier grizzly bears?

What sporting events come to mind? The Iditarod Trail Sled Dog Race? Skiing, hunting, fishing?

How about inline skating?

Imagining all but the latter, I prepared for a writer's conference in Alaska by calling skating publications and looking up clubs on the Internet. Could I skate there? Where? All pre-adventure research reaped consistent results—"no information available." Alaskan-based skate clubs responded to my cyberspace queries with "transfer interrupted" messages.

"Do people skate in Alaska?" This initially seemed a reasonable question until the tenth time I asked it. A "Yes" response eluded me. I decided to take my skates anyway.

I initially packed for my excursion as one would for any trip—incorrectly. Luckily, my friend Sal had won the Iditashoe—a snowshoe race held in Anchorage—and offered apparel appropriate for the uncertain weather conditions there.

She layered my body with enough clothing to open an outlet. From the waterproof hat, to a jacket with zippers galore, three pairs of pants of varying thickness, gloves, socks, scarves, shirts for under, over and in between—I was attired for any climatic upheaval. I wondered where skating fit in the picture as I peered into her full-length mirror and observed a multi-colored Pillsbury Dough Babe. The only thing between me and my Calvin's was three additional pairs of pants. Speed of any kind was out of the question. I lumbered forward with my legs spread out to accommodate the material between them.

A day later I stood on the curb at the airport and loaded myself and three fat bags into the Holiday Inn shuttle. The driver informed me that Anchorage has a paved inline skating, biking, and walking trail, spreading about 112 miles around the city. The part used mostly by skaters is the Tony Knowles Trail, eleven miles in length, with other trails feeding into it. During winter months, it is used for cross-country skiing.

Coming from the 105-degree weather of Sacramento, California, I could feel the striking drop in temperature. I layered fabric over myself and strapped on skates. Bravely rolling from the hotel lobby into the parking lot, I was mentally prepared to face wolves, elk, and extreme weather conditions. A mere fifty-nine degrees whisked across my face, turning my cheeks red. Looking towards town, I headed for the trail. My arms were open, ready to embrace Alaska. There was so much material surrounding them, they could not rest at my sides, anyway.

The only Eskimos apparent were figurines in store windows. A modern city with tall buildings but a hometown feel, Anchorage is known as the "Hanging Basket Capital of the World." Baskets of flowers suspend from old-fashioned street lamps providing explosions of color on that late September day along the city's storefronts. Grateful to experience a piece of the world I would miss if I did not skate, I contentedly glided through the largest city in the largest state in the Union, manipulating around curbs and kinsmen.

I found the trail and skated along an inlet. A mile ahead, leaves from thousands of trees—yellow, red and amber—enveloped portions of the course. At times they blocked out the sun, darkening the pathway. Rounding a curve, a sunny park with acres of grass and a lake framed by snow-capped mountains in the background popped into view. The route weaved past schools and connected to neighborhoods and other trails at times by wooden bridges, where my skates would "ker-thump, thump, thump." Detonating into flight, a flock of geese abandoned a trailside pond, honking in commotion. The sky instantly filled with them, and almost as fast, they became absorbed into the skyline. Their noisy departure faded with distance.

Bob and Sharon Washington were skating for the last time that season. "Next week those mountains will be covered by snow." Bob confidently pointed to three of Alaska's thirty-nine mountain ranges. He seemed certain of his forecasting abilities. "We will be cross-country skiing here by then." Bob and his wife Sharon, both in their forties, skate every summer. The three of us traveled together for two miles until they departed into one of the neighborhoods. "By the way," Bob cautioned, "if you see a moose, don't try to pet it." He was quite serious. Imagine, in California I tried to avoid squirrels and dogs, but never anything bigger than a Doberman.

I continued along the inlet. This same trail could take me past the airport, parks, into thickly wooded forests, past the University of Anchorage, along bodies of water ranging from creeks, ponds and the Captain Cook Inlet in addition to many parts of town. I did not expect to find this trail or the beauty surrounding it—especially in a state with over 100,000 glaciers where mussing dogs are not uncommon and grizzly bears can be observed from one's seat on the bus.

The very next day, it rained, hailed, and snowed. Within twenty-four hours, snow covered the distant mountains, making Bob's prediction a reality. My prediction that skating in Alaska would pose problems was replaced by the reality of smooth trails, glorious sights and excitement. I experienced magnificent Anchorage in a way made possible only because I had inline skates. I am grateful for the day of skating before the storm and that instead of packing my former stay-put-frumpy-thinking for this trip, I carried a skate bag instead.

Holland's T-Stop Through the Tulips Tour

She spies on us, undetected by my fellows, though lashes as thick as a comb's teeth. I know she is watching. Her eyes, the size of quarters, travel left to right, right to left, tracking the next one of us that appears, then disappears down the narrow trail, swallowed by tall grass. The cement path slices through thousands of lush, green acres interrupted only by intermittent windmills and barns seemingly as old as the land. She watches without moving her head, though her black and white ears occasionally twitch, one at a time. Perhaps her wet nose smells our next oncoming intruder who moves past her without taking steps the way the farmers do, but glides smoothly like ducks rolling on a concrete pond.

It was not wooden shoes that lured me to Holland, it was inline skates. With more bicycle paths—"Fietspads"—than roads, one can literally bike—or skate—across the entire nation. Legal everywhere, inline enthusiasts are welcome to share trails with two- and four-legged beasts including cyclists, pedestrians, horses, sheep and cows. Make that cows with a capital "C." They come in multitudes, at times spreading out as far as your sunglasses allow. Close your eyes and picture thousands of black and white beasts. No, you are not in front of the wallpaper at Ben and Jerry's—you are on a bike trail in Holland.

This time my skates took me farther than ever before— over an ocean on a nine-hour flight to Amsterdam for an inline skate tour, the company's first. The orga- nizer, Allan Wright, launched an American skate tour com- pany called Zephyr, with in- ternational destinations. Its

maiden voyage commenced in the Netherlands.

Every few years I do a marathon skate in memory of my mother's fight with breast cancer, to raise money for cancer research and pro- mote resource awareness for families of breast cancer victims. These resources did not exist when my mother contracted the disease during my childhood. There was no one to talk to. I felt alone and frightened. These days kids can be matched with same-age chil- dren so they do not face having a parent with cancer without some- one to talk to in the same situation. Someone who really knows what it is like.

I had already skated the length and width of California for the above reason. The Holland tour would give me the opportunity to skate across an entire country—or at least miles equal to the length— for the same cause. Better yet, someone else would map out the route and make hotel reservations. It sounded snazzy to tell folks I was scheduled to skate across an entire country when in actuality the California roll of 1400 miles was much longer than The Nether- lands' three hundred.

Our group met in adrenaline-charged Amsterdam described by a fellow skater as, "It is like New York; there is so much energy you just want to honk your horn."

Allan mapped out two daily routes, one for the long distance skaters and a shorter route for the rest of the group who covered about twelve to eighteen miles a day for seven days. I joined the short distance skaters in the morning then took off on my own, meeting up with them at night before 7:30 p.m. dinner.

Allan looked me in the eye every day and said, "You will never get lost if you just follow the map and the directions." His thirty-one-year old face, young and handsome, repeated this theory with sincerity but I got lost every afternoon without fail. One day, determined not to get lost, I read my map with extra caution, comparing it to the signs along the trail. One big sign read: "Makkum—8 kilometers." Eight kilometers and 1,000 cows later another sign: "Makkum—16 kilometers." Each night got me where I wanted to go, just not when.

The first few times I was lost my mind raced. "Why didn't I bring a better map? Why did these directions make sense until I got to the sheep crossing grate and the two windmills? Do cows bite? Do they chase skaters as dogs do? Will a 'bad guy' jump out from behind a parked tractor? Why can't I remember the name of the night's hotel or the town it is in?" Why? Why? Why?" Each morning we rose early, enjoyed a generous breakfast and started skating while I was still in a daze. The details of our daily destination did not seem that important until I was up to my eyes in cows with no human in sight.

Being lost in a land where you speak no more than two of the native words is a good teaching tool. Ego, embarrassment and the "I'm-not-going-to-ask-directions" attitude are useless unless you want to sleep on the ground. Sometimes sparsely scattered farmhouses were the only roofs I saw, hour after hour. It almost became easy to skate up a long, concrete driveway, knock on the door and look lost. Standing there in my Bicycles-Plus T-shirt and dirty inline skates, the homeowners somehow knew. "American?" they would ask.

They read my mind—right through my helmet. A blizzard of words came out of whoever answered the door and people would magically appear. I could not figure out how to express "lost again" or their word for "W C"—water closet, (the last day I learned what it is—toilet!) so I would look especially pitiful. It was not much of a stretch. The blond-haired, blue-eyed Dutch men and women would come to the right conclusion every time.

Smelling like the cow pies I skated through, they welcomed me to roll over their meticulously scrubbed hardwood floors to wash up in perfectly clean bathrooms in homes so charming they look like artists' renderings for Country Cottage Magazine. It felt good to be in Holland. No matter how lost and frustrated I got, I knew instinctively that someone would help me and I would not have to sleep with the bulls and goats, lucky for them.

Traveling so many miles on paths as narrow as two feet or as wide as ten, be it alone or with the group, the cobwebs and concerns of everyday life flew right out of my head. Monday through Friday commotion makes room for the endless miles of green countryside with villages and towns made of brick and cobblestone. Some buildings were thousands of years old, like ones in Amsterdam which were undoubtedly looked upon by Pieter Van Maren, my great-great-grandfather, before he brought the family genes to California 150 years ago.

Dynamic local individuals added dramatically to our adventure. Dutchman Willem Cornelius Augustine, a seventy-four-year-old resident of Hindeloopen, dazzled us with charm and skate form. Willem is a nine-time participant of the internationally famous Eleven Cities Race, known as the Elfstedentocht—a 200K ice skate race. He competed in two during the Nazi Occupation of World War II before being jailed and eventually sent to a concentration camp, then a labor camp, by the Nazis. After the war, he participated in additional Elfstedentocht races.

Willem gave us instructions on how to position our bodies for best speed, endurance and performance. He swept past windmills, story-book-like villages and through the vast countryside with its hordes of ever-present livestock which lifted their heads to watch him float by under skies as blue and playful as his Jack Nicholson eyes.

Willem explained how the Elfstedentocht runs only when the ice is thick enough to accommodate the weight of thousands of skaters through eleven cities, connected by the canals they skate on. "It has been held only fifteen times since it began in 1909, with twenty-two at the first race." The most recent race was held on January 4,

The road to paradise is sometimes paved in poop.

1997, with 16,731 skaters. The Elfstedentocht winner becomes an instant national hero.

On one occasion, a smiling gentleman approached the support van after noticing the Zephyr Inline Skate Tours sign on its side. A few hours later the group was gathered around coffee and tea at the home of Pieter Kamstra and his family, in the small town of Wommels. Kamstra is the founder of the inline version of the Elfstedentocht. It commenced in 1988 with twelve participants and eventually grew to hundreds.

Kamstra's quaint home lies next to a canal that freezes every winter providing a playground for his ice skating "habit." Just inside his entryway hanging from the walls and ceiling were the tools of this habit —over one hundred pairs of skates including antique, modern, ice, and inline varieties. "He's as crazy as you are, Suzan," offered an anonymous voice.

Kamstra solemnly noted, "In 1997 there was an Englishman who had a black band on his head. At noon he stopped skating for one minute of silence in honor of Princess Diana, whose funeral was held at the time of the race."

The experience of skating across a nation taught me much about my own. Taking jaunts in memory of my mother feels as if she is introducing the world to me, as she did when I was small. Whether you skate for distance, speed, a cause, your country, or adventure, there is plenty of room to do it in The Netherlands.

Indianapolis Babe 500

This Indianapolis tourist waits and watches. Perspiration creeps from beneath my guide's helmet and slips over his eyebrows and off his nose. It plops past his lips and chin splashing atop kneepads below. He seems not to notice as he speaks of monuments and soldiers lost and how his city does not forget them. His hands are wrapped in black plastic with holes cut out for the finger he points at an old building that once housed his great-grandfather's business. The aged building is momentarily renewed through his reminiscence. The history of the city pours out of him like the waterfall making a path down his face. I wonder.

Where does all this water come from?

Heavy air with its sidekick humidity pulls sweat from tour guide and tourist like a vacuum sucking dust up from carpet. This same moisture serves to cool us as we float down streets and cracked sidewalks chronicling centuries of architecture mixed with the anecdotes of a fourth-generation resident. This rolling review exposes Indianapolis' past, present, and future hopes through the eyes of forty-three-year-old Matt Rota-Autry, Indiana University Purdue University at Indianapolis's (IUPUI) Director of Intramural and Recreational Sports. He knows his city's history as well as his own, sharing both as we maneuver curbs, sidewalks, loose bricks, and each other. This city tour of Indianapolis needs no tour bus, just inline skates.

The tour this day starts at IUPUI, where Matt teaches an elective course on inline skating. His one-credit class provides instruction in beginner, intermediate, and advanced skills. Once wheeling with zest and stability, students are treated to four *tour du jours* composed of city routes of varying lengths and destinations. Matt's students skate in "real life" downtown conditions while simultaneously schooled in the city's history, architecture, commerce, and curb approaches and descents. Today's route is a 9.5-mile combination of all four tours.

The city is a mix of new and old. I do my best to navigate around its workers, residents and automobiles. Employees awaiting the bus near the Capitol Building acknowledge us with friendly nods. Most everyone we encounter does. We pass fountains, endless war memorials and in the city's center, Monument Circle—the original site of the governor's house in 1821. The downtown home was built in 1827, but the governor's wife did not want to hang her laundry out for public display. It allegedly served instead as a brothel and was eventually demolished, becoming a pasture. It is now 342 feet of limestone with stairs leading to its tower with a glass-enclosed balcony at the top providing a view of downtown. In the basement is a museum of Civil and Spanish American war mementos. We can not see the museum but pause to admire the 38-foot bronze statue of Victory (or Miss Indiana) while placing a hand under a huge brass buffalo, whose mouth spouts water at the base of the steps.

Whiffs of fries, hamburgers, and waffle cones emanate from fast-food places tucked tightly between downtown businesses. The "shake" part of "Steak n' Shake" sounds like a fine thing to place against a hot forehead, until stepping down and up a curb, around a mailbox, and carefully between pedestrians before maneuvering a right turn on a green light behind Rota-Autry. He monitors traffic road conditions as he glides effortlessly while mixing a story about the Federal Building with a warning about an approaching car.

More parks, fountains, monuments, and anecdotes lead to Pan Am Plaza with its flapping flags snapping applause at us. All 50 states are represented. I learn that only one state flag is not rectangle—Ohio's. It is in the shape of a snake's tongue.

Two and a half hours from the start, the sojourn ends near Canal Walk, a renovated 10.5-block downtown canal that has become a center of activity on the West Side of town. Paddle boaters part through smooth canal waters under an occasional spray from the fountain in the canal's center. The lights of the city twinkle from the skyline making paths of bumpy white and yellow over water stirred by the little boats. Children dance over sunken spotlights throwing gigantic shadows up onto a statue.

I peruse Matt's inline skating class syllabus, which contains tour routes, course rules, safety gear requirements, tour sights, historical descriptions of buildings and landmarks and a glossary of skating terms, which include:

TANKED—Poor skating performance

BACON IN THE PAN—When you wipe out and slide around then shrivel up like frying bacon.

ROAD PIZZA—Sand, rocks, gravel, sewer grates, unleveled pavement, and other hazards that can contribute to a fall.

GRILL—Face or facial features.

DOME—Your head.

AIR—What you "catch" when jumping or bashing.

"Bashing" sounds intriguing.

"What is it?" I inquire.

"Skating down stairs."

I closely examine Rota-Autry's face. Little gray and brown whiskers poke out of his face. Ever-present sweat from ninety-percent humidity still rolls off his nose. He is no teenage wonder boy with an empty "dome" but a respectable, tax-paying adult owned by a dog named Maya Angelou. Better still, he is old enough not to do

something stupid. I conclude this because … he is my age.

A coward avoids fear; a brave person faces it. So does a knucklehead. It is my chance to expand my skills under the watchful eyes of an expert.

"Show me," I challenge, trying to sound nonchalant. We schedule a meeting for the next day at high noon.

The obstacle "course" consists of three steps in White River Park near the canal. Only three little steps. Already a master of gliding off curbs, I tell myself, "This simply adds two more." My stocky legs, conditioned by skating on steep California hills, suddenly become gelatin. Make that soup. I face the steps without grace or style but with a splat. Matt encourages and compliments me as I eye the cement with no sense of affection or trust. The city beyond fills the skyline with buildings and clouds that reflect down onto the canal waters. The beauty of the spot offers no consolation. I head for the steps again, then again. Four times in a row, I "wimp out" at the last moment and jump over all three, landing upright, with a vigorous wobble.

Matt cheers, but I do not hear him. Instead, I hear the imaginary cracking of my aging bones. My next attempt ends in a plop. I pick myself up promptly and sneak a peek to see if anyone has witnessed my folly. My dignity takes a little longer to leave the pavement. There is a just little scrap on my leg and shoulder. My kneepads serve me well. I skate away, turn, and advance again, noticing a few people watching. This time the steps have grown deeper and more threatening; and my arms go up as I go down. (Glossary term: "Touching God.") Some of my skin lies at the bottom of the steps, but I can't quit now. More people pause to watch my bravery.

"Just relax," he encourages.

The last time someone said that to me, I was in my twenty-second hour of labor. Then too I faced tremendous fear, pain, and a desire to do away with all witnesses.

Twelve imperfect bashes completed, the quest for perfection somehow got mangled with the quest to rescue dignity. With a deep breath and prayer, I finally successfully ride down the three cement monsters, rolling smoothly and upright on the landing. Thank God above. Instead of savoring victory, I vow to keep my big mouth shut the next time I happen across a word I do not understand.

What I do understand is that Indianapolis holds more than the corn, clouds, and race cars that I envisioned. The nation's twelfth largest city has a revitalized downtown that boasts a merge of history entwined with modern updating. Skating through Indy's downtown or surrounding Greenways that connect 57 parks and 125 destinations is enough to prompt me to step out of my skates and stay awhile. Tomorrow I will visit the State Capitol building, and take on the steps without fear or hesitation, in my Nikes®.

Switzerland's "Feel-the-Love" Tour

"Do you feel the love? Can you feeeeeeeeeeel the love? SIR! How 'bout you? MA'AM! Ladies and Gentleman, can you feel the love?" Well-built, muscular arms beckon the crowd to draw close.

Fifty pairs of eyes lift up from three-inch-thick omelets, French toast the size of a quarter loaf of bread, and overflowing salads decorated with edible flowers. He stands by a long wooden table flanked by benches topped with men and women donning colorful helmets and rolling footwear. Flowers spill from pots suspended from lattice that shades the connecting street-side cafes lining the stone road in the Italian part of Switzerland. Our eyes dance with expectation as we await the crowd's reaction to our tourmate. He is at it again. We exchange clandestine smiles.

I watch strangers jolted from their brunches and table talk in French, Italian and German—three widely used languages in Switzerland—silently study our big man. English blasts out again, only a little louder. "Do you feel the love, miss?" He motions to an elderly diner. His tall frame is hoisted higher on a pair of well-used inline skates. If she spoke English, she would know the wit of Butch Quick, a New York graphic designer, is as swift as Eddie Murphy's and his smile as contagious. His companions know it. We have covered hundreds of miles with him along Switzerland's Rhone River

Valley, through ancient cities passing centuries-old castles to the sound of melodic church bells and clanking, tinny cowbells. We have enjoyed many lavish dinners with him in the Valais area, home to Europe's largest valley glacier, experiencing cuisine and restaurants so different from home. We've recaptured the day's sights, sounds, and smells over wine, fondue, and dried horsemeat most of us heartily enjoy—until someone blurts out what it is—all to Butch's outbursts of friendliness and ever-flowing invitations for the locals to join in and *feel the love*. Sometimes they do. Mostly they stare with their mouths open. Grinning restaurant and hotel owners sometimes take pictures of the fray, or ask to be in one. Butch always recruits a local to snap the shot, of course.

If food, scenery, surprises, and people define great adventures, the roll along the Rhone had it all. We came from three countries and converged in Visp, a charming little town with few tourists, for another Zephyr inline-skate tour. This time my skates rolled me directly into the pages of a book—Switzerland—where I glided along

Our guide Andrea Franklin appraoches our first wire bridge.

a river roaring beside me under the cool shadow of the Alps. The Alps. It was only six years earlier that I could hardly find my way out of my own backyard. That is, until I came face to face with the ultimate means of escape—urethane wheels.

Our group begins as strangers and quickly grows inseparable within days. There are three each in there 40s, 50s and 60s, plus two in their 30s and a 27-year-old. Remarkably, the 50- and 60-year-olds ultimately lead the pack throughout most of the tour. One of two 66-year-olds, Don Larson, discovered rock climbing a few years earlier. There was no stopping him from suddenly catapulting his lanky limbs up a mountainside or over a wire bridge that stretched above roaring, foaming green waters, wearing his five-wheel inline skates all the while, naturally. Bleachers were no match for him either.

"You learn to live with it," Susan, Don's wife of forty years, told me one day. "I never know what he's going to do."

Neither did the group and we enjoyed the anticipation of Don's next vertical effort. It was as impossible to contemplate what he would shoot up next, as it was to predict Butch's next outburst of love. Neither kept us waiting long, much to our delight.

The tour brochure suggested using skates that cost $180 dollars or more. Those with cheap skates or ones over three years old should consider upgrading. Neil Hindle brought cheap skates and was rewarded with a prize-winning blister the diameter of an orange by the second day. Sabine Lowenthal, an East German native who owns a Swiss inline skate park with her husband, guided us the first three days and lent Neil a pair of quality skates. All guides were experts at wrapping hurting feet and he managed quite well from then on. Though his blister had a life of its own for weeks, they could wrap it in such a way that it did not bother him though it was a ghastly sight indeed. He was happy to send me a picture after the tour was over, bragging about the progress of the purple pancake attached to his instep.

Our three guides spoke German, French, and English. Since English is not widely spoken in Switzerland—which actually adds to the fun—it was nice to have Pennsylvania's French-born Isabel Greenberg to dispel the mysteries of menus or translate what the locals were saying about us. Andrea Franklin, an extraordinary skater and writer for *Fitness and Speedskating Times*, was the tour's

Don's roller mountain/bridge climbing shoes

Don Larsen goes over the bridge his way. The Rhone River roars below.

ever-lively American-born counterpart.

We got at least two meals a day and a morning meeting where we discussed the day's routes. There were usually three of varying lengths from seven to thirty miles. The entire group usually did the short route together. After completion, some took the support van to the next town and others opted for an additional ten to twenty miles, maps, and "adventurous directions" in hand. Two women in the group cycled on this "bike-friendly" tour. (Not every family is lucky enough to have two skaters.) I usually did the medium route but opted for the longer one once or twice. Unlike Holland, I was not collecting miles so I stayed with small groups and enjoyed the feeling of not being lost with someone who spoke the native language near by.

Worries about one's ability to stop were abated by the mostly flat or slightly downhill surfaces. The guides were all International Inline Skating Association Level II instructors who gave tips on stopping plus numerous other techniques during optional daily clinics. The best part about learning something new—like how to get more mileage out of each stroke—is practicing it immediately on our daily routes with the guides giving us tips as we glided.

Despite ceaseless coaching and group support, one participant defied all stop-technique training—a self-proclaimed mad scientist, thirty-year-old Dr. Neil Hindle, an Englishman residing in Rotterdam. The guides helped him over the rough—or steep—spots, though he did have a knack for defying gravity and taking off on perpendicular paths. He paid much homage to Mother Earth by going down on all fours on every corner. He once disappeared into a descending black abyss—an underpass that opened at the bottom of a hill into a sharp turn.

"The face of a local cyclist as I came around the corner through the tunnel is a memory that will stay with me," says Hindle.

I found myself more than once braking for him as I held him by the seat of the pants on the downhill, but you won't hear me complaining.

One day a curmudgeonly owner of a three-story house with balconies of bountiful blooms beckoned us to sip his homemade wine—red and white.

"Very fresh indeed," stated Neil, himself a chemist, though his efforts reaped him a Ph.D. instead of a basement filled with wine vats.

We passed thousands of neat, long rows of pear trees, apple orchards, and vineyards that climbed and weaved from the road to the mountaintop like cornrows in a woman's hair. The steep grade gave the illusion that they could fall off at any moment. How were they watered? If one forgot to turn off the hose, would he flood everyone below? Cow and sheep bells spilled music down the mountain. The trail zigzagged into a field of corn at least seven feet high, which swallowed the lead skaters who eventually reappeared near one of many well-kept graveyards generously anointed with abundant bouquets, lanterns, and ornate headstones with pictures of the deceased. One had an eighty-eight-year-old woman whose 105-year-old mother followed her in death by six months.

Switzerland's many fountains provide refreshment for weary skaters

We traveled over streets as wide as meadows or so narrow we could extend our arms and almost touch buildings built centuries earlier. Doorsteps often separated front doors from the roads. Blossoms burst from windowsills stacked up in rows of seven, ten, or higher. We passed an old woman stroking a stone doorstep with a stiff homemade broom. Two glides after that a bakery beckoned us to wrap our faces around fruit-covered pastries too beautiful to eat, appearing as if crafted by artists. Three strokes beyond, dozens of tables emerged with menus displaying brightly colored little balls of ice cream, about five to eight to a bowl. The most eagerly anticipated sights were the plentiful fountains, the size of troughs that offered ice cold mountain water, with flower baskets hanging on stone posts. The spout was usually a human or animal head beautifully crafted out of brass or copper. The vivid beauty and enchanting discoveries rejuvenated my essence that had been lagging a bit before the trip.

The support van took our baggage to the next hotel each day on the seven-day tour, and we followed by skate, van, boat, or train. On our last roll we took a boat across the clear turquoise waters of Lake Geneva to Montreau. We then headed for Gstaad in a window-roofed train. A blast of green towered over us as we traveled past rural residences, with horses, sheep and cows leaning into the countryside. We wondered if their legs were different lengths to accommodate the deep slope. We were suspended with mountain and sky above and below us.

Gstaad looks like postcard Switzerland with its snow-covered Alps and chalets with profuse flower baskets. We hiked from there and enjoyed a "mountain meal" of endless entrees, breads, and wine. Cooked entirely over a wood fire, there was no electricity that day on the mountain. I recognized horsemeat as the main course and said nothing. No one would have minded after sipping the 90% proof Schnapps served with the meal. Naturally, wine flowed as it always did on our European treks. We ate and gazed at a home across the gorge flattened by an avalanche the previous winter. Single homes cannot be on parcels less than forty acres so there was plenty of mountainside between the scarce houses. Back in Gstaad, we explored its 50 shops, 30 restaurants, and some visited a casino while others sought out the salt water pools. It is a favorite of the rich and famous. Liz Taylor had a 3-million-dollar asking price on her vacation chalet. The group pooled a down payment that would reap no more than a box of crackers.

Pennsylvanian John Goushian said, "Being a veteran of two skates I thought I'd know what to expect. All that went quickly out the window once we hit the roads of Switzerland—I was lost in the scenery."

Indeed. The landscape defines Switzerland with the Alps always visible from literally every angle. One participant said what he'd remember about the trip is, "Skating over wire bridges with views that always include a 360-degree view of mountains that look like velvet green turtle necks wrapped around the throats of snow capped mountains with collars made of cotton clouds." You get the picture: Swiss scenery is a buffet of beauty whose splendor leaves you breathless. So does following a pack of skaters who encase their hinnies in tight and bright stretch pants. As they say about Switzerland, the scenery alone is worth the trip. Go there, and *feel the love.*

Writing about skating not only led to articles in newspapers and magazines, but also the Internet. Here is one written for GoNomad, *an adventure travel webzine.*

Sneak up on a Horse in Intercourse (PA)

Twelve questioning eyes study him. He rests on the edge of a field that evaporates into the horizon beyond the road. No one blinks from behind the window of a home scrubbed clean long before it ever becomes dirty. The stranger runs his hand through freshly tilled soil, turned by a team of horses that pulls the family plow. He takes in the distinctive smell of the earth and the scent of freshly mowed hay. Cautiously, the mother and her five barefoot children draw near 'The English.'

"Why you doing that?" the three-year-old blurts.

"Because it's fun," he answers.

The woman pulls the child behind her 19th century dress as if to say, "Don't talk to strangers." Richard Barnet's inline skates have transformed him not into a foreign country but a foreign century.

Calorie-burning-breeze-over-the-knees perspectives of new destinations are replacing margarita-by-the-beach vacations for some. Richard Barnet, Professor of Recording Industry at Middle Tennessee State University near Nashville, is one of twenty-five participants of an inline skate tour of Pennsylvania's Amish Country. It commences in Lancaster County known for many things including a town called Intercourse, located next to a village called Bird in the Hand. Blue Balls is further down the road.

Barnet at first frets that his fifty-year-old body may not make the grade. His fears are dispelled the first day as people of all ages, body types, and physical conditions gather. Their anticipation hides behind twenty-five pairs of sunglasses.

Allan Wright, the tour organizer, advises them to remember to enjoy the scenery and ask permission before snapping a close-up picture of the Amish, who embrace an austere life style, shun technology, and ride in horse-drawn buggies. The group learns that the three-day tour provides routes that accommodate beginning, immediate, and advanced skaters. A support van tags along and folks "in need" get tips on braking and other techniques by International Inline Skate Association certified instructors. One guide is Amish, who will answer questions about his culture.

The days fly by and so do covered bridges, massive white farmhouses, restored colonial homes, and cows lazing in the sun. When silos silhouette against twilight, a home-style Amish meal awaits the rollers.

The last tour day falls on Sunday. After church lets out, Barnet recalls dozens of horse-drawn carriages progressing slowly onto the roads. A short time later, he realizes he is sandwiched between two lines of carriages—twenty ahead and thirty behind.

He sums up inline tour benefits: "The music-like sound of two hundred horseshoes on the blacktop roadway as children strained to see "The English" with rolling shoes shall forever stay with me."

Grab yourself a memory that will last forever. Sign up for an inline-skate tour, and experience a whole new world under your feet. After all, it's not every day that you can skate through Intercourse.

Silly fun is for everyone.

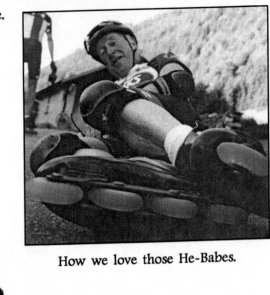

How we love those He-Babes.

Babes love to feel the fresh air
swooshing over their helmets.

5

Testimonials

Don't take my word for it. Though I insist you believe everything I say, herein lies the experiences of a He-Babe, a Babe, and a He-Babe-in-Training.

Inline Skating and the Weekend Dad

Being a weekend dad has always been a challenge. How do you get in quality time with your kids when it is your weekend? My three youngest children Nicolette, Dustin, and Renny, who are ten, eight, and six, discovered it a year before I did. It was something we could all do on an equal level. Having been a distance runner, I had always dreamed of a day when I could run with my kids by my side. The problem with this picture is long-distance running is not recommended for children their ages. Their bone structure is still too soft to withstand the impact of long-distance running. With inline skating, my children's little feet are rolling on wheels rather than pounding on pavement. The impact on their young bones is minimal. The new picture I have is the four of us inline skating on summer evenings at the local supermarket parking lot. We also go to local inline-skating events and participate, side by side. This is heaven for a weekend dad and the best part is it is something we can do right now. Inline skating has given the four of us a wonderful weekend activity that we look forward to whenever we are together—and for me that is what it is all about—being together!

Inline Skater Forever
Frank Marsh,
Northern California

75

A letter from a friend:

Finally bit the bullet, heaved this old body out of the chair in front of the computer and got myself on inlines for the first time - now I understand all this enthusiasm! What a kick. Three friends and I (in the mid-forty to fifty range) rented skates and took a beginner lesson (actually, pre-beginner—or maybe fetal, but charity prohibits my characterizing it as such) from Liz Miller. The biggest brag we had was not our grace and form, but that not one of us fell down—other than then Liz had us do it on purpose to test out our padding—the rented kind not the God and living applied kind!

We had such a good time and came away with such an exhilarating sense of accomplishment—mind you we skated on the ultimate flat surface, but everybody has to start somewhere, right?

You definitely got me fascinated, thank you, I'm just a slow starter, but now there is no stopping me—skates for my 50th the end of this month!

Reggie Winner, Editor
California Hockey and Skating

How to Get Your Rightful Share of "F" — An Executive's View of an Inline Marathon

As Director of California's Small Business and Professions Agency, I know what is important in life: increased productivity and the bottom line. "Show me the money" is my motto. My world starts at my desk—everything is in order and run with perfect time management. I have a system for everything and my system works. I tell my employees, my children, and my ex-wife to approach life as you would an office—state goals, stay focused, catalog everything, then run with the ball. Do not dally. There is no time for rose smelling or tree hugging. There is a job to do and the satisfaction of doing it well is worth the sacrifice. That is your reward.

Imagine my shock when I went in for my annual review. I predicted accolades, progress charts, and even applause. To my dismay, my new boss, Miss Carol Marrell, a girl in her thirties, wrote across my evaluation—lighten up. Put a red "F" on your calendar once a week. I was stunned further (but somewhat relieved) when I learned what "F" meant: *FUN*.

My mind whirling, I stepped back. What was she talking about? This was life, not a game.

"Take a seat," she pointed a long, pink fingernail towards the conference table. It was the first time I noticed she wore expensive rings on several fingers, though her wedding finger donned a large opal, not a wedding band. The cuff of her finely tailored navy blazer pulled up when she stretched her arm, revealing clanky bracelets that banged against each other. She smelled faintly of roses.

Child, recreation and aggressive skates cover the individual needs of the Team-Babe.

"The new management strategy is to create fun and team building in the workplace; both escalate productivity. I believe you need to stretch your paradigm and be open to new ways of doing things and allowing your employees to do the same." Her auburn hair bobbed around her shoulders as she spoke. I knew she was feeling her UCLA MBA, but fun over finance? Fun over leadership? What possessed this woman? Surely more time and experience with the Agency would straighten her out.

"So where do I find this *fun*?" I humored her.

Noticing the doubtful tone in my voice, she straightened to her full five feet, two inches and suggested I join several office employees at an inline skating event in the Bay Area. It would commence in Napa and end in Calistoga located twenty-seven miles up the road. I bravely rose to the occasion without a whimper. Picturing reckless people with obnoxious hair to compliment the rings in their noses, I knew what to expect, but my *modus operandi* is "never turn down a challenge from the boss."

"Fine" I said, "See? That starts with an 'F.'"

She smiled and said nothing.

Over the next week I listened carefully, extracting information from conversations of employees registered for the event. I was unnerved to learn that people I supervise were actually going to do it. Enthusiasm mixed with nervousness oozed from Elizabeth Best. Mrs. Best had big hair, a big chest and a big behind. I tried to imagine her feet in something other the high heels she always wore, but could not. Mrs. Best waddled when she walked, as her high heels clicked all the way up and down the marble hallways. I did not know if it was her tight skirts, or pointy shoes, but she moved from side to side when she went forward. Albert Deda, Elizabeth's former supervisor from the Public Information Office, looked too tall, too thin, and too gray to even consider this excursion of "F," but he too was going. He had held his job through six administrations. Since that had not killed him, maybe this would.

"They are all too old to try something so foolish and dangerous," I thought, wisely keeping this to myself. After work, I headed straight to an all-night bookstore and coffee shop to enlighten myself. I read skating magazines and perused inline skating books. Determined to do things the right way, I learned the terms of the sport. I even glanced at some triathlon books where crazy people swim, bike, and run many miles regardless of high or low temperatures. I knew my knowledge would enable me to be a leader among support people, which was my assigned position.

The day arrived, and promptly at 6:30 a.m., in the parking lot of the Budget Inn on Redwood Street, in Napa, California, I made my appearance. The brochure clearly stated that registration started at 6:30 a.m. but I was the only person exactly on time. There were sleepy "twenty-somethings" sitting behind card tables that bore "REGISTRATION" signs. A dozen unpacked boxes loaded with event T-shirts were behind the tables along with piles of free water bottles for the participants. Crisp and white, the shirts featured a skater gliding past big, purple grapes with *Roll Through the Wine Country* on the back. I wondered how

I could get my hands on one without being seen. They looked good on the volunteers.

Completely ready and prepared, I considered my upcoming duties: drive along the course providing water, first aide, fruit, bagels, plus anything else our staff required, during their long trek up the Silverado Trail. Miss Marrell forgot to say something about picking up the staff when they gave up, but I was prepared for that too. The mini-van's seats were clean with all seat belts in position—some retrieved from under the cushion. Miss Marrell took me aside. Had she not spoken, I would not have recognized her under the purple helmet with "Girls Rule" skating stickers. She was fully outfitted in skating paraphernalia—wrist and elbow guards, kneepads, and skates of course. I stared at her with my mouth open, but just for a moment, then caught myself and looked at her with my full attention. She held out something.

"This is what we call the Pee-Can. Keep it in your van. Don't throw it away. Some of our women may need it."

I had read that many athletes do not seek out Shell Stations during long races. They exit the course and relieve themselves right there on the side of the road. Modesty often leaves an athlete in competition the article stated, and it was no big deal. Miss Marrell did not want me to be surprised if I saw this, but I assured her I knew all about it. No way could I imagine the gals from our office using a gas station bathroom much less squatting on the side of the road. It was not a pleasant thing to envision but seemed a reasonable compromise to employ a "Pee-Can," which sounds like pecan as in pie. I held my breath and coolly took the can, which was actually an empty Big Gulp container from 7-11®.

Miss Marrell asked me to meet the skaters at the official starting point, two miles away from the registration area. The skaters, all suited up in the Budget Inn parking lot, would skate there as a group after registration closed.

"Park close, but not too close. Some may need to use the can."

Showing her I was a team player, I showed no resistance to her request. My eyebrows remained in place though I was dying to roll my eyes at her.

"Easy enough, you can count on my support," I smiled as I said it. She was wearing a tank top and black nylon shorts. In a million years, I would never have imagined having a boss that looked like that. She caught me looking at her.

"Don't let all that starch around your collar give you a rash." She smiled when she said it. Naturally, her comment startled me a bit. I found it to be a little too playful.

As she glided away in what looked liked rolling ski boots, I realized that about fifty skaters had gathered during our conversation. They formed long lines at the registration tables or conversed with other participants. Many glided slowly through the expanding crowd, or fastened race numbers to their clothes with tiny safety pins. I spotted Angelica Dalebout and Betty Brown, both secretaries from Data Entry. Angelica looked great for a woman in her fifties. She wore the oversized T-shirt she received at registration. It was white with a pair of inline skates set inside a large orange circle. The shirt's back read *Napa to Calistoga.* Her legs looked long and lean under her black leggings. Mother Nature had not been so kind to Betty, although she was ten years younger. Betty's skate shirt pulled up revealing extra-wide thighs wrapped in black stretch pants. She was two inches shorter and two times wider than Angelica. Both wore gigantic smiles under their helmets, laughing at themselves and each other. They did not even notice me.

Twenty-five minutes later an announcement was made about *not* skating in the middle of Highway 49, but staying on the side of the road during the race. Precisely at 7:08 a.m., it was time to head for the starting point.

The skaters glided through town, past closed bars, gas stations, and sleeping strip malls. Skaters ker-thump-thumped over railroad tracks and stopped at red lights in a glorious display of colorful fabrics. They occupied the right-hand lane and shouted to each other, "Car back! Car up!" They spread out but still resembled a consolidated unit as they swept along. The experts assisted the less-experienced skaters. You could tell the novices or doing-it-for-fun skaters because their clothes were not as fancy, and their skates usually had four wheels instead of five. Those five-wheel skates were amazing to look at. Wearers would slide one long skate on its side behind a gliding one—an impossible feat of balance to my mind—then stop. I was waiting for a fall that would down the group like a parade of rainbow dominos.

The skaters came to the final intersection connecting to the Silverado Trail—the official starting point. Their dazzling skinsuits announced, "Look at me in these loud colors!" without using a word. These people were not what I expected. They came in all shapes, sizes, and ages. I knew they felt ridiculous in those outfits. I also suspected the material would ride up uncomfortably during the race, pinching them in places they would not want pinched. It was for looks, I concluded. I wondered how many were gay.

Five minutes before the race, I spotted my boss. She raised her brows to acknowledge me. Perhaps she needed something, but I was not sure. There were at least a hundred skaters between us. Was it time for the Pee-Can? I moved quickly to retrieve it. Determined to show her that I could follow directions to the letter, no matter how odd they were, I returned, holding the container up high so she would notice. In response, her eyebrows shot up in a show of utter dismay. I wondered what her problem was *this time*. She and other racers stared at me. Miss Marrell's mouth was actually open. She looked at what I was holding and I suddenly understood.

"Oh! Do you need it now?" I shouted, over dozens of colorful helmets. I struggled to get close enough to hand it to her but she backed away, her eyes holding a crazed look.

The group of skaters around her looked at me, looked at the Big Gulp waving over my head, looked at each other and back at me. How can all these people in space suits give *me* a funny look? I thought. Suddenly, I understood. Miss Marrell was in the middle of a sentence and I must have interrupted. She was my new boss after all, and clearly, my intrusion was inappropriate. Unaccustomed to taking directions from a woman, especially a young one, I respected her position.

I decided the skaters around her should know there was more to me than my new sporting attire with crisp white shirt, matching pants and Nike® logo. I was doing my job and I knew what I was doing. "I'm in charge of potty privileges," I revealed to several men and women ranging in age from about twenty to sixty. Turning to my boss I said, "Miss Marrell, want to use this now?"

She beckoned me to follow her as she skated far from the ears of her fellows. "What are you doing with *that*?" she hissed. "We discretely use it in the car! I can't believe you offered me a gigantic Big Gulp container to fill with urine, right in front of two hundred people!" She seemed amazed, but sincere.

"You said the can was in the car, not *used* in the car," I retorted. I reminded her that "in the car" did not connote "used" in the car. I was ready to stand my ground, but her expression told me it would be useless.

The countdown started, and the skaters readied to roll. I watched them take off and admit to feeling a little impressed. I approved of the way the Pro Skaters, competing for money and equipment, started first. The men took off and a minute later, the women. Shortly after that the citizen class or recreational skaters departed. This provided structure and organization, which I liked though I did not know why they did it.

I got in the van and traveled a few miles ahead, waiting for the thirteen people from our office to appear. I stood on the side of the road holding nine fully loaded water bottles. I learned something: complete strangers skate by and take them! Didn't they know this water was *not* for them? The organizer's support people held water out for everyone, but this was for *my* team. No one seemed to consider this as they zoomed past, grabbing a bottle, chugging the water and throwing the container onto the side of the road. "You bring that back!" I shouted a few times. The same thing happened to the grapes and bananas I held out.

About ten miles down the road Betty and Angelica came by, thanking me enthusiastically for the bagels I handed them. They were already carrying bananas. Someone else's bananas. I discovered pulling over on the side of a hill was not practical because skaters could not stop, nor did they want to, on the downhill. My job was not easy. I thought my skaters would stick together. I observed their faces as they passed. The closer they got to Calistoga the deeper their grimaces.

"Never catch me doing this." I confirmed to no one in particular at the fifteen-mile mark. Vineyards spread out all around me—lush, rich and green. I relaxed in the presence of this beauty mixed with the unanticipated adrenaline rush I got when one of our own came into view. I wondered why they did it. Perfectly sensible, productive office workers wearing those dangerous inline skates was bad enough, but to go through this was nuts. Feeling a gentle breeze, I relaxed and admired the view while thoroughly enjoying my own sanity.

Miles increased and paces slowed accordingly, but their faces remained fixed with determination. "Want to quit? Get in the car!" I offered to Fran Westsmith, a fifty-one-year-old grand-mother and fine administrative assistant from the Legislative Unit. She continued to stride past, giving me a nod. I suspected she would take me up on my offer in a mile or so.

I made the same offer to—and got the same response from—everyone in our office. Even Ed Drennan dismissed me with a nod of his black helmet that exposed wisps of snow-white hair. I realized it was Ed only after first spotting a basketball-shaped, lycra-encased orb, coming straight at me as I stood on the side of the road. Bright blue and red fabric stretched tight over the gut no doubt maintained by the steady supply of Hostess Ding-Dongs that he kept in his desk. He looked ridiculous in his Bikes Plus/24-hour Nautilus cyclist jersey and matching tights. I bet he thought he was big stuff that day.

About two hours after the start of the race, our first skater crossed the finish line. Cheering wildly, finishers stood on both sides of the street showing their support of the other skaters during their final moments. Former grimacing faces broke into smiles with each final stroke. Many removed sunglasses to reveal eyes that seemed illuminated from behind. The race's first place finisher came in at 1:18 (one hour, eighteen minutes.) Our fastest skater finished in 2:06, our last at 3:01 and the very last two skaters came in at 3:30 and 3:31. Close to 200 participated.

The race over, the skaters gathered at a Calistoga park. What a mix. The removal of helmets revealed some of the wildest hair-dos I ever saw. A friendly guy name Zack had hair clipped and shaved to resemble a soccer ball. Every other octagon-like shape was shaved down to his naked skull surrounded by patches of longer hair colored in bright pink, yellow or florescent orange. Naturally, he had matching goatee. No one treated him like he was weird, which he looked to me. Zack fit right in with the doctors, lawyers, seniors and others who had endured those long miles. Joyfully conversing, they loaded their plates with potato salad, pasta, watermelon, and barbecued chicken. I felt a tinge of envy. They had a bond between them regardless of age or how different they looked from each other. They were a solid unit bonded together by the love of skating and the accomplishment of participating.

They asked about each other's times. I thought their low scores would embarrass the slower skaters. What could feel good about finishing in163rd place? Yet, each face brightened as times were exchanged then compared to last year's event. How different. It suddenly occurred to me they were competing with themselves, not each other. They kept harping on how wonderful they felt just for showing up. Several people said, "If I can do this, I can do anything."

One gal said, "I feel like I can face my new job with renewed confidence, even without much experience. I will hang in there like I hung in here." Other testimonials resonated the same concept of conquering self-doubt in an intellectual area, now that they had taken this physical and mental challenge.

I thought about that for a long time.

On Monday, the office buzzed with tales about the race. "Congratulations" became the word of the day. The entire seventeenth floor had raised spirits. I learned that goofy-looking Zack is featured every night in Jay Leno's Tonight Show opening promo, kicking a soccer ball on his inline skates. Of our office skaters, Miss Marrell finished second to last. This did not seem to bother her at all. People were clearly energized by the excitement she exuded when she spoke of her quest.

Several planned their next Napa to Calistoga coming up in two months, with still another in two months after that. Secretly, I contacted an outdoor sporting goods store and arranged to rent skates and take lessons. There was no way I was going to get stuck with the Pee-Can again.

— George Compleeka, New Babe Extraordinaire

Part Two
How~To

Once you've tried being a Babe on Blades,
everything else seems out-of-date

1

The Inline Advantage

Time to get on with it. This how-to section will give you every-thing you need to get started. Even if you have been skating for years, review these techniques. You will learn something. If you are really advanced, don't forget to study the *Special Skills for Babes in Need* and the *Skate by Antics for Bad Babes* towards the end of the book. Let me know what happens.

Getting Started

You want to be better, bolder, and bouncier. You look at yourself and say, hmm . . . how can I ever ignore the fat cells multiplying around my inner and outer thighs and feel good about myself all at the same time?"

Can you make a purchasing decision that helps push away the sins of your life without surgery? Y-E-S. Treat yourself and pull out your wallet and buy something that will make you feel so good, others will want to feel you too—a pair of inline skates. Tell yourself, or someone who loves you who has a credit card, skates are as the Spice Girls used to say, what you "really, really want."

Here is the strategy to get yourself, or a loved one, *to lay down the money:*

Extol the fitness benefits of inline skating. The health benefits of exercise are undeniable. Exercise gives your circulation, metabo-lism, and brainpower a huge boost. It sharpens the mind, making Babes more competitive in the work place. At one time, some Babes thought they would be retiring at fifty. These days, many women this age have children in elementary school. Exercise helps us take on the world instead of being overtaken by it.

Inline skating is a wild and wacky way to work out *and* it is good for you, unless you roll into a Doberman pinscher or a parked car. But you are too smart for that because you will take a lesson and learn how to stop *at will* instead of *by prayer*. Check out the International Inline Skating Associations (IISA) web page at www.iisa.org to find a certified inline skating instructor in your area. Prepared with the basics, you will take on the neighborhood with zest, confidence, and fewer shrieks.

Brag about the calories burned per half-hour—about 300. Compare it to cycling and running, inline skating at a steady, comfortable rate for 30 minutes will produce a heart rate of 140-170 beats/minute and calorie expenditure of 285-310, about 10 calories/minute. This compares to 320 and 360 calories burned for running and cycling, at the same heart rate, respectively. Interval skating—alternating one minute of hard skating with one-minute moderate skating burns 450 calories per half-hour. Mentally, mood rises with exercise, so you will be less of a Grinch—a real plus for people who live with you.

Point out the aerobic benefits of inline skating compared to cycling or running. The faster one skates the higher one's aerobic activity. This energizes the way the heart and lungs work together to bring oxygen to the heart. Inline skating tends to be a better workout in this respect than cycling, but a lesser workout than running. This is simply because cyclists can coast and runners cannot—no gliding on your buns for runners, and hopefully not skaters.

Anaerobic benefits determine how well muscles are strengthened and developed by a workout. Babes want to burn fat, not muscle. When diet alone without exercise is used to reduce weight, women can lose muscle tissue, sometimes as high as 40 percent of their total weight loss. Exercise combats this.

The low impact of skating compared to running means that the sport does not render the pounding of hip, knee, ankle and foot joints that running can. According to a University of Massachusetts study, it causes less than 50 percent of the impact shock of running, making it less stressful to the joints. Bottom line, if one wants to lose calories and simultaneously develop muscle tone, inline skating is a gloriously healthy way to do it.

If muscle building is important to you, note that a study conducted by Minnesota's Human Performance Laboratory at St. Cloud University discovered that inline skating develops muscles in the rear end, hips, lower back and the entire upper leg. Swinging the arms during skating develops muscles in the upper arms and shoulders. You won't look like Popeye, but you won't look like Olive Oil either.

Babes looking to build balance find it with inline skating. Humans, including Babes, lose balance as they age. Skating increases balance significantly. This helps us age gracefully, like a Babe.

Inline Skating is fun and comes in many flavors such as: recreational, fitness, aggressive, speed, and hockey and freestyle skating. No matter what style of inline you chose, good things await you. Get out your VISA® card. You deserve it. Do it for fun. Do it for yourself. Do it for all those second helpings you sneak when no one is looking. Did you think we hadn't noticed?

2

Choices, Choices, Choices

As a Babe on Blades you need more than solid will, daring, and attitude. You need stuff. Cool stuff. The most important piece of equipment is your helmet, then skates and safety gear. Once you collect those items from retailers, your next contribution is your body. Your attitude combined with the above equipment will enable you to take on the tarmac... then the world.

Inline Skates

Some look like ski boots with a hard outer shell and others look like overgrown tennis shoes. They come in men and women's styles. The shape of a foot is called the "last," and women's and men's lasts are as different as the rest of their bodies are from one another. Do not buy a skate that is "unisex" because it probably is a man's skate made smaller with extra padding and then called a woman's. That is like taking men's underwear, making it smaller and calling it women's wear. The shape is just wrong from the start.

Inline Skate

Rollerblades®

What is Inline?

Inline skates have wheels that are in a line. Roller or Quad skates have wheels side by side, two in the front and two in the back. Some folks think inline skaters move in a line. Babes do not necessarily travel in nice straight lines but scramble in all directions. Many folks call inline skates "rollerblades." Deduct two points from now on if you call this vehicle to freedom and adventure a rollerblade. Rollerblade® is the successful company that got the public all stirred up about inline skating. Thus, the term "rollerblading" was born. Saying "rollerblade" or "rollerblading" is like calling a photocopy machine a Xerox® or gelatin "Jell-O®." Everyone on the earth knows what you mean, but it is "politically" incorrect. Its use is so common, it may find its way into a dictionary some day, as many popular slang terms do.

So how can we call a woman on skates a Babe on Blades? Isn't this politically incorrect? Babes don't worry about being politically correct. That's what makes us Babes. Besides, we've gotten thousands of grown-up people to try the sport of inline skating who had not considered it before. They thought it was for kids. It is. It's for the kid in all of us.

Skates come in many styles, as do skaters

Before You Head for the Store

At the moment, you are wondering where to go, what to buy, and how much to spend. I know this because I can read your mind behind your sunglasses. Before you rush to the store, you must determine your skating needs. What type of skating do you want to do? Some skates are for playing hockey, others are for zipping along at thirty miles an hour, and others are for riding down hand-rails or flipping backwards while defying gravity. Most Babes want recreational skates. They want to glide, not flip or fly.

How to Buy a Skate

Finding the Skate That Will Best Serve the Feet of the Babe Goddess

Like men, all skates are not created equal. They come in all price ranges and there is a wide range in quality worthy of a thorough investigation. In buying a skate, first determine the style of skating that interests you. This book is for recreational skaters—those who want to do it for fun, exercise, and mischief.

Determine Your Style

Styles of Skates and Skaters

Recreational Skaters make up the largest portion of the 33 million-plus inline skating population, which includes kids of all ages—

Recreational Skates

Race/Speed Skates

from two to eighty-two. They are the folks you see almost everywhere, sometimes screaming with pleasure, and sometimes just screaming. Recreation skates come in hard and soft boots; some have buckles, laces, Velcro® straps, or a combination.

Fitness/cross-training skating serves as a cross-training tool to strengthen and maintain muscle tone during the off-season for other sports, such as skiing. Similar to recreational skates, these puppies are often lighter, have a low-cut boot and larger wheels. Fitness skaters are out to burn fat and calories and keep in shape. If you are a man, please skip to the next paragraph. Women: you will like what this does to your own buns and inner thighs, but don't forget to be cheeky and take a good, long gander at the buns of a He-Babe as he whizzes past you on his recreational or fitness skates. Some high-end recreational skates are used as fitness and cross-training skates. It is hard to tell them apart although their components may differ.

Speed skates have five wheels, a longer frame, and the boot is often low-cut and leather. Speed racing teams exemplify the sport to its maximal professional level. Speedskates are usually not available in sporting good stores, but specialty shops. Race skaters are in it for speed. They typically look like gods and goddesses in Spandex. Their lycra-covered bodies have not one wrinkle from neck to knee. They are usually experienced skaters and it is an experience to gaze upon them.

Production five-wheeled skates have five wheels like speedskates

Colorful child in child skates, grown-up in production five-wheeled skates (photo by Betty Brown).

Hockey Skates
(notice there is no
brake!)

but are pre-assembled and heavier. They are used for recreational and long-distance skating. Chosen over four-wheeled models because of the longer wheelbase, they give a Babe extra oomph with each stroke, carrying her a little farther. These skates are more stable at high speeds but harder to maneuver than four-wheeled skates.

Roller Hockey, one of our nation's fastest growing sports, appeals to youths and adults alike with hockey leagues exploding all over the United States. These skates are similar to ice hockey skates and lace up for a close fit. Their wheels are constructed for very quick movements. These skates often do not support the ankles of new

Aggressive or Vert
skates, note the
small wheels and
no brakes

skaters. They are great on the glass-smooth surface of a rink, but don't stand up well to the gravel and potholed outdoor world. Roller hockey was originally used for off-season training for ice hockey players. Today the sport boasts millions of players, most of whom have never stepped foot on the ice.

Aggressive skaters are the guys and gals who "grind" rails, go down steps backwards, defy gravity and generally annoy grown-ups. These skates have small flat wheels, grind plates on the frame and no brake. They are built for extreme use so the wearer can slide, flip, spin, and who-knows-what on ramps and half-pipes. The skates, wheels, and protective gear of this group must be extra heavy-duty to withstand the rigors of the sport. Spectacular to watch, aggressive skating gets much media attention.

All-terrain skates are off-road (or off-pavement) skates introduced to the market a few years ago. They have gigantic wheels that look like mini-bicycle tires and are less common and pricey.

All-terrain skates (photo by Dan Graydon)

Picking out the right skate can boggle the mind
(photo by Stephen Brown)

3

Buying Basics for Babes

Comfort, Quality, and Price

Now that you have determined what kind of skating you want to do, determine what is most important to you—comfort, quality, or price.

Most first-time Buying-Babes want to spend as little as possible on their skates because they are often not informed about high-quality skates. With the idea of "trying out a sport" without too big of an initial investment, the novice may find herself nailed to the tarmac. This was this author's approach lo many years ago. If you don't want to pay much for your skates, you will skimp on comfort and quality. Low-end skates are made with low-end materials resulting in low-end fun. Cheap skates result in little ankle support, achy feet, lethargic bearings, bad wheels, and a bumpy ride. Many of my students come to class in inexpensive skates and quickly notice that they can't keep up with their classmates. For most, it is not the skater's lack of ability, it is the skate that prevents them from gliding easily. I point out to my students that in a better product, the student would find the class drills much easier and darn more fun.

Skates come in a wide variety of prices. This Babe thinks a good skate can be purchased for $150 or more. Really great skates range from about $180 to $300-plus dollars. This is retail price, not sales price. Many Babes have spent less and gotten great skates because of closeouts or clearance sales.

As a rule, the more money you spend on skates, the better off you will be in the long roll. If you buy crummy skates made with cheap components, you won't skate for long. If your budget is $50, go to a discount or toy store and pick something bright and bold. You will not skate on them for long, so you need to make a fashion splash up front.

When you purchase skates know that if they do not feel good in the store they will feel worse on the road. Do not accept "They will conform to your foot over time." If they hurt when you buy them, they will feel worse after an hour or two on the roll.

Basics for Buying-Babes

- Rent—It is best to rent first, and take a lesson in your rental skates. You wouldn't buy a car without knowing how to drive, so if you can, rent, take a lesson, and then purchase your first pair.
- Going to specialty sporting goods stores, asking certified instructors and peers such as skate club members about their opinions on their skates is a great way to find out information.
- *Never* buy your skates in a toy store. Naughty. Naughty.
- Don't forget to factor the cost of safety gear ($35–$60) plus helmet when estimating the total cost of your adventure. If gear seems expensive to you, try to estimate what you might spend on one hospital trip.
- Wear the socks you will be skating in when you try on skates. Remember socks designed for athletic endeavors are best because they help wick the moisture away from your feet, which reduces blisters and keeps your toes smelling like a rose. At least that's what we claim.
- Go to a sporting goods store and cross-examine the employees. Ask specific questions such as, "Can you show me how to remove my wheel or replace the brake?" If they cannot or will not answer, keep your money in your sports bra and head for the door.
- Learn as much as you can about the skates that the store carries. Take notes jotting down specific brands and models, then go to another store and repeat the procedure. Beware of stores that have a limited selection, or you'll get a load of hype about what they have and not what YOU need. Interviewing employees about skates will educate you and help you determine whom you can trust and where you will

buy. This effort is well worth it and will serve you well.

♦ Try the skates on and skate around the store if they'll let you get away with it. Remember that it is better to apologize than ask permission. Why risk hearing that awful word *"No"* if you can avoid it? Many Babes actually enjoy hearing a call over the store's loudspeaker, such as, "Will the woman in the red shirt please roll back to the skate department?"

♦ Never buy skates without trying them on, but of course, you know that.

♦ Ask the staff if replacement parts for *your* skate are available. These include wheels, bearings, and brakes.

♦ Go to a local park or places where people skate and ask other skaters. Skaters love to talk about inline skating, so don't be shy.

♦ Many stores apply the rental cost towards purchasing a new pair. Ask for an additional ten percent discount. Keep a straight face. You'd be amazed how well this works for many. This act alone, no matter what the answer, qualifies you as a real Babe.

Remember: *Don't* buy cheap kid stuff in discount stores. What works well for a kid won't work well for you. You don't "bounce" like a kid. They have latex instead of blood rushing through their bodies, plus, you weigh more. You are a grownup, at least according to your birth certificate, so buy quality product for grownups.

DON'T—It's not always better the second time around.

Never buy used skates with trashed wheels thinking that you will save money by buying new wheels. You will spend from $40–$90 on wheels, from $25–$60 on bearings, and another $20 or so on spacers. So, just put that cash into a good quality pair of skates, and you will be miles ahead and have money left for a double cappuccino on the way home.

Well-Worn Wheel

Sure, they are cute on her, but you need skates designed for YOU.

Kids' vs. Grown-up Skates

Though it is often hard to tell the difference, grownups are bigger and have drivers' licenses. When it comes to skates, there is a big difference. Kids' skates are usually under $100 and some are much less. They are made for children and not grownups. Adults will roll slowly and perform poorly in kids' skates. You will not have much fun, your feet will hurt, and you will become cranky.

Discount Stores vs. Specialty Shops

Babes need attention. They deserve it and sometimes demand it. Discount stores cannot service our bearings or adjust our tootsies. They cannot replace parts or do a little doctoring when the skate patient needs a tweak or adjustment. They can offer great discounts but so can specialty sporting goods stores. It is a trade-off. Know that once you purchase skates you are on your own with a discount store, though that may be just dandy with you. I prefer to deal with experts because my feet like attention.

Women's Skates

Better manufacturers offer models built specifically for women. Her calf muscle is lower than a man's and her Achilles tendon is narrower. Women-specific skates are built with these features in mind. Don't buy a man's skate with a thicker liner. It can't compensate for your heels and calves.

Remember: If your skates don't fit, you will eventually have a fit. Skates that hurt today are candidates for next year's garage sale. Comfort is key.

Skate Fit Tips

Heels and Toes—Stand with your skate laced or buckled. Your heel should be snug in the heel cup and your toes just barely touching the front of the boot. Wiggle your toes. Bend your knees. The pressure should cause your toes to pull back slightly. Squished toes are bad and so are loose ones.

Buckles—With buckles and/or laces in place, make sure there are no pressure points. Adjust the buckles, straps, and/or laces to evenly spread support over your entire foot. Some folks with high arches will benefit from an arch support that sells for about $30. Avoid skates that put pressure on your arch. This results in sore feet later.

Flex—Skates with laces offer more flexibility, but buckles are quicker to get in and out.

Movement—Forward flexibility is important in balance. Lateral stability is crucial in confident striding and gliding. Lateral flexibility in hockey skates allows for quick turns but is counter-productive for a recreational and fitness skater who needs stability in the ankles.

Remember:
- There should not be any pressure at the widest part of your foot (your skate is too narrow). This will eventually cause pain.
- Your heels should not slide away from or around the heel cup when you bend your knees. Loose heels cause blisters.
- Never buy skates with the idea that they will "break in" like tennis shoes. You want a snug fit with the ability to move your toes.

Next up: necessary gear!

HAVE-NO-FEAR SAFETY GEAR

Babes are Well-Equipped and Properly Protected
Protective gear is not optional.
You need it.
It will benefit you.
Put it on and stop whining.

Women's Specific Protective Gear vs. Unisex
Some companies make gear designed especially for women. Have you ever noticed that men are sometimes shaped like barrels over chicken legs, and women are shaped like pears? Well, the rest

Women-specific product is a
favorite of many Babes.

of a woman is different from a man (what a revelation) and there are wrist, elbow, and kneepads made to accommodate our curves. Even you can't find women's gear, (be warned, sizes tend to run small) make sure you buy good quality *adult gear*. Children's gear is great for children, but it can scoot off an adult body during a fall. The weight of an adult demands equipment engineered for those forces. Don't squander safety for frugality by purchasing yourself kid's stuff. Remember, Babes are not cheap—at least that is what we claim.

Wrist Guards

Your hands and wrists are the most likely parts of you that will get injured in a fall. These guards have strong plastic pieces on the underside to protect you from collecting pavement in the palms and enable you to slide instead of plop.

Elbow Pads

These will protect you, especially if you fall backward.

Knee Pads

Your knees will be better off in falls when surrounded by these. Pads also help you get up gracefully in grand Babe style

Good Things Come in Small (and Large) Packages

You can buy wrist, elbow, and knee pads in a single packaged deal or separately. Different sizes of protective equipment may be required on your particular unique and spectacular frame, Babe, because you may not be the same size all over. This hearty Babe is a medium in some places and a large in others, so prepackaged gear does not work for me. Make sure you try on your safety equipment before you find yourself in a park, anticipation high and ready to roll, only to discover your gear does not fit properly. This happens to my students. They come to class with recently purchased gear that is too tight or too loose.

Helmets

Skate helmets have no particular requirements that make them different from bike helmets. The most important thing is to get one *and always wear it*. A quality helmet is key. It should be American National Standards Institute (ANSI), Snell (Snell Memorial Foundation) or American Standards for Testing Materials (ASTM) approved. Look on the inside of the helmet to make sure there is a sticker denoting this. Without one of these approvals, the helmet does not meet the high standards for maximum protection required by Babes.

The above three groups independently test manufacturers' helmets. They establish specific helmet standards for motorcycling, equestrian sports, bicycling, inline skating and skateboarding, snowboarding and skiing, and for other sports. These standards address performance and protection, not looks or design. They upgrade their specifications on performance characteristics of helmets to keep pace with advances in materials, helmet technology, and design. You now know why Babes crave their approval— at least for their helmets.

Some aggressive skaters buy helmets that protect their foreheads and the lower part of their necks. These look very cool when you are upside down and six feet in the air. Since most Babes prefer to be right-side-up with wheels planted solidly

Helmet head is what they say. The joke's on them, it hides the gray.

105

on the ground, a standard style helmet, properly appointed with stickers, works great. Remember that your head is the one part of your body that you can not replace.

Since Babes like to keep cool on hot days, it is important to make sure your helmet is properly vented. Many helmets are sold with no or few vents. Your head will cook like a baked potato if your headgear is not vented, and your tongue will hang out like an old hound dog's. It is worth a few extra bucks to get the extra venting to be comfortable. Babes deserve it!

Padded Pants—Power Buns

Many Babes ask about sporting padded pants just in case they fall backwards. Rather than rely on the false security of padded

pants, improve your technique and learn how to fall correctly. Still, many women consider this option especially if they have had a prior coccyx injury, or if they are nervous about falling when they are new to the sport. Some members of the latter group reject the pants after seeing their foam-encased backsides in a mirror. For people obsessed about the size of their buns, these pants generously embellish what one already has. If your strong sense of confidence allows you take on the world in padded pants, why not?

Clothes

Loose and comfortable is a must for Babe skaters. Jeans do not give the flexibility you need like stretch pants or shorts. Some Babes like spandex, while others prefer loose

Padded pants maximize
natural padding

cotton pants. What counts is that you feel comfortable and unrestricted as you joyfully glide down the promenade, insects bouncing off your Cheshire grin.

Lights Out—For Our Glow in the Dark Babes

Night gear is important for obvious reasons—when it comes to vehicles, you want to be seen, not felt. Let them observe you coming and going. Wear light-colored clothing with reflector straps. Helmet, waist, and skate night-lights are ideal—hook them in several places. Night lights can be set to blink in a variety of ways and can be attached by elastic straps or clips. These can be found in most sporting good stores—often in the bicycle section

Sock It to Me

Many experts recommend avoiding cotton socks because they hold moisture next to your feet. Cotton is absorbent, but there is no place for the water to go so your foot sits in hot moisture during long skates. Athlete's foot may result. Some skaters like double socks that are ready-made with a two-layer construction. This helps prevent blisters and "hot spots" that occur when your socks rub against your feet. Some folks feel double socks make them slip in their skate boot, others like them. It is an individual decision.

Many skaters recommend a thin liner sock of polypropylene or silk that wicks moisture from the foot and cuts down on friction between your skin and the skate. They wear these under an athletic sock of medium weight. There are specially padded athletic socks designed with a thicker heel and toe especially for inline skates. These work poorly for me because my skates fit so well, a thicker sock makes my skate too tight. I recommend a sock with polypropylene of medium thickness. Sporting goods stores, including cycle and marine shops, carry this specialized clothing.

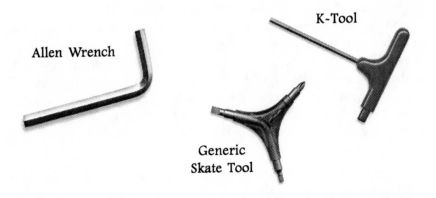

Allen Wrench

K-Tool

Generic
Skate Tool

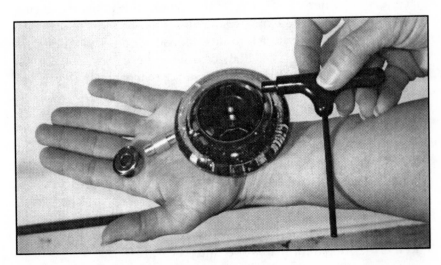

Bearing, Spacer and K-Tool (photo by Hur Alvardo)

Nuts and Bolts

Spacer

Bearings

4

Skate Parts and Maintenance

Keeping your skates in good shape pays off and is easy to do. First, let's look at what the Babe skate is made of.

Parts of a Skate

- *Boot (or shell)*—The part you put your big foot in.
- *Soft vs. plastic boots*—Soft boots look like big tennis shoes and are usually supported by an exterior plastic cuff. Made of lightweight materials, they are lighter and more form-fitting than plastic boots.
- *Hinged cuffs*—Support the ankle and allow for forward flexibility.
- *Buckles*—Easy to get on and off and adjust on the "roll." Babes with arthritic fingers sometimes prefer buckles.

Strap (some skates have buckles)

Laces

Soft boot

Standard heel brake

Brake pad

Frame

Nut

Wheel

- *Laces*—Permits a more tailored fit. Most skates have both buckles and laces, which allows for maximum custom fit.

- *Vent*—Allows for breathability and airflow. If a boot has no vents, your toes will feel like slow-cooked hard-boiled eggs.

- *Liners*—Found in plastic boots and can be removed, washed, or replaced.

- *Insoles*—High-end recreational skates have removable preformed arch supports. If you don't like the ones that come in the skate, you can get arch supports separately at sporting good stores.

- *Frame*—The part attached to the boot and wheels made of plastic, nylon, or aluminum. Longer frames accommodate more wheels. Aggressive skates often have "grind plates" attached to the frame. This allows testosterone bearers to glide along curbs and park benches as if by magic.

- *Standard Brake*—Retails for about $6. Don't leave home without it.

- *Cuff-Activated Brake*—A mechanism on the back of the skate that forces the brake downward from the pressure of a skater's calf when she pushes her braking foot forward. It can be raised up as a skater's ability increases.

- *Wheels*—Wheels come in all shapes (or profiles), sizes, and degrees of hardness. The larger ones roll faster and the smaller ones are good for stunts.

The IISA offers the following information on inline skate wheels:

Size—The diameter of the wheel has to do with its size at the widest part, measured in millimeters (mm). Larger wheels roll longer and therefore move faster than smaller ones. Most recreational skates come with 72-76mm diameter wheels. Lower-end recreational skates are usually equipped with wheels that are 70 mm to 72 mm. These smaller wheels provide a lower center of gravity, something new skaters like because they are just a little closer to the ground. High-grade inline skates come with wheels up to 82 mm, which provide a faster roll.

Hardness—Wheels are made of a plastic material called urethane, with varying levels of hardness. This hardness is measured on a

Aggressive Wheel

Recreational Wheel

Wheels!

durometer which is indicated on the wheel with an "A," with 0A being the softest and 100A the hardest. Softer wheels make for a smoother roll but wear out faster than harder wheels. Most recreational skates have 76A to 82A wheels. It is easy to confuse wheel size (mm) with durometer (A) so if you do this, don't get kahslepped, it happens.

A softer wheel gives you greater "grip" on the pavement. Harder wheels last longer but make it slightly harder to grab the road. Look at the wheels that come with the skate. When it is time to replace them, decide if you like the hardness and purchase accordingly.

Bearings—The wheels roll on ball bearings, which are inside the hubs of the wheels. Most wheels have two bearings, which enable them to spin. Higher- priced skates use bearings that are rated (Annular Bearing Engineering Council) ABEC—1, 3, 5, or 7 with 7 being the most precise, though it makes little difference to a beginning skater.

Skate Care

Skates require little care. Check the wheels every week to see if they are wearing on the inside edge and need to be rotated. Otherwise, keep them clean with a damp cloth or brush. Some Babes enjoy appearing in skates with mud splashed over the frames. It makes some feel like road warriors, which they are.

Wheel Rotation

Rotating your wheels makes them last much longer. When you notice that the wheel is wearing on the inside, change the first to third, second to fourth, and remember to switch the outside of the wheel so it now faces the inside. Wheels wear from the inside because we push off on our inner edges when we glide.

When changing your wheels, hold the skate firmly between your legs. It is best not to wear a dress with nylons for this procedure. Use your trusty Allen wrench to remove the bolt. An Allen wrench is the little L-shaped hexagonal metal bar that comes with a new pair of skates.

Remove the first wheel first. Then remove the third, flip the wheel over and switch places. Then go on to two and four. The

Wheel Rotation

wheel under the brake usually has a longer bolt. Don't mix this up with your shorter bolts.

No Cheating...

Some skaters just rotate the first wheel when they see it wearing. Soon the front wheel will not touch the ground like the other three wheels. **Babe Renelle** did just this and when she *finally* rotated her wheels properly, the front wheel became the third one and did not touch the ground at all. She felt sheepish, but being a Babe, she got over it.

Replacing Wheels

Take your skates in. You would not buy a tire without taking in the car, would you? If you purchase wheels without the skate, your new wheels may not fit in the frame that holds them. Consider the surfaces you travel. Rough roads wear wheels faster, so you don't want to purchase wheels that are too soft. Those work better on the smooth maple in a skating rink. When your wheels are dinky compared to when you first purchased your skate, it may be time to replace them (see page 101 for an example of a well-worn wheel). If you rotate them regularly, they should last several months or more, depending on frequency of use.

Bearings

When bearings are clean, they spin well. When they are dirty, they can cause you to move very slowly or not at all. Most bearings

Taking off a wheel

will last a long time as long as you avoid water and dirt. Many women buy new bearings when the old ones are dirty and not spinning well, others enjoy spending a few relaxing hours cleaning them and making a big mess.

Give Yourself a Brake: Changing Yours

Your brake needs to be replaced when it has worn down about two-thirds of the way. Some people replace theirs half way; others wait until the bolt is exposed (not recommended). Take your skate with you when you purchase a new brake to make sure it will fit properly. Some brands of skates do not accept brakes made by other manufacturers or even the same manufacturer of a different model. If the store has a service department, have the technician assist you the first time you do it. Otherwise, secure the skate and remove the nuts and bolts with an Allen wrench. Some models will require you to remove the last wheel.

Brakes can be moved to the left skate if you feel more inclined to use your left leg to brake. Some brakes cannot be removed at all, or require a technician.

Brakepads, the one on the left is new, the right used.

Brakepads, used on left, new on right.

Lessons can boost confidence

5

Safe Sailing–Rules of the Road

Inline skating is basically a safe sport. Having a lesson and wearing safety equipment add dramatically to reducing injury. That, and common sense, will get you far. The most important thing is a safety-conscious attitude by playing it safe in the beginning and sticking to skating on flat surfaces with no traffic until you are comfortable using the brake. Leave the hills for later.

Lessons will teach you proper stances and how to fall without injury. My students just love it when they learn they are going to fall in class. Okay, they do not initially embrace the idea when I fall without warning and slide a few yards just to get their attention. It works.

This book will show you the basic positions that you will learn in a lesson, but I urge to you take one. The dynamic of having an instructor keeping an eye on you is powerful. Those who sustain the most injuries are children, no surprise. They skate more than adults and are more likely to not wear gear including wrist guards, which could prevent the most common injury in inline skating—a broken wrist. Still, your most important piece of equipment is your helmet because head injuries can be fatal.

To see the most up-to-date information on inline skating and safety statistics, check out the International Inline Skating Association (IISA) web site at www.iisa.org. This site answers frequently asked questions about safety ranging from the most common cause of falls (the answer is hazardous road conditions such as potholes), to the effectiveness of safety gear (it really does work), how lessons help, plus injury rates compared to other sports, and more. The site changes regularly and is the greatest single source of inline skating information available today. See **Appendix A** for more information about this organization.

RULES OF THE ROAD

Safe skating is a snap when you remember to SLAP!

Skate:

Smart

Legal

Alert

Polite

Skate Smart

- ◆ Always wear your protective gear—helmet, wrist protection, elbow pads, and knee pads.
- ◆ Master the basics—striding, stopping, and turning.
- ◆ Keep your equipment in proper working order .

Skate Legal

- ◆ Obey all traffic regulations. When on skates, you are subject to the same laws and obligations as a bicyclist or a driver of an automobile. Different counties have varying local laws.

Skate Alert

- ◆ Skate under control at all times.
- ◆ Watch out for road hazards.
- ◆ Avoid water, oil, and sand.
- ◆ Avoid traffic.

Skate Polite

- ◆ Skate on the right, pass on the left.
- ◆ Announce your intentions by saying, "Passing on your left."
- ◆ *Always* yield to pedestrians.

Now that you're safely equipped and you know
the rules of the road, you're ready for the next step!

Is there anything the well-equipped Babe can't face?

6

Things to Avoid

Water

Oil

Sand

Gravel

Drains

Pedestrians

Poodles

And, of course, people who own poodles... scary!

WRONG! Use more than just the straps if your gear comes with a "tube." Some do, some don't.

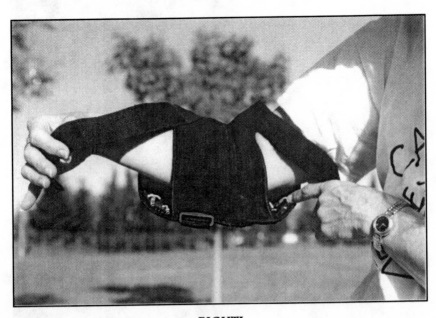

RIGHT!

Let's Get it On

My strong girlfriends! It is time to get it on. Rip those pads out of their packages, break out the box that houses your helmet, and don't forget to grab your skates while you are at it.

Have a seat. You may gear up on a bench, the carpet or the grass, but do not let me catch you putting your skates on while standing up. When you try to balance yourself on one foot that has wheels under it, while trying to ease your toes into a "wheeled shoe," you are asking for a plunk on the pavement. Babes cringe when they think of the sound of their buns meeting the roadway, especially in front of witnesses who claim not to be as foolish.

PUT ON THAT GEAR, MY DEAR

The last things you will put on are your wrist guards. Once they are in place, it is too hard to sign autographs, much less use your hands for anything else. Start with your elbow pads then put on your knees pads, helmet, skates and finally wrist protection.

Elbow Pads

These protect your elbows should you fall backwards. Wear with the plastic pointing out- ward. Many skaters acci- dentally wear them upside down. Make sure the name of the manufacturer is right side up.

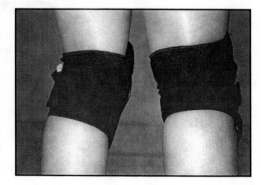

Knee Pads

If the brand you buy has a fabric backing, slide it up your leg like a tube—

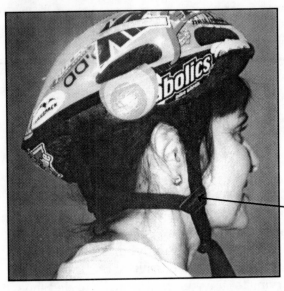

Make sure the "do-hickey" is directly under your ear (yes, that is its technical name).

don't just wrap the strap behind your knee. This procedure reduces the impact of a fall and keeps the guard on your knees if you slide a couple of feet.

Helmets

A common mistake is that people wear their helmets too far back, which won't do your forehead much good if you fall on your face. Make sure the straps are secure under your chin—almost too tight feeling—and the adjusters are fastened directly under your ear lobes. They should not hang down like the ears of a basset hound. A bike helmet works just fine.

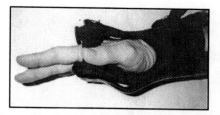 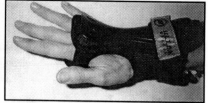

Make sure the curve is on the bottom

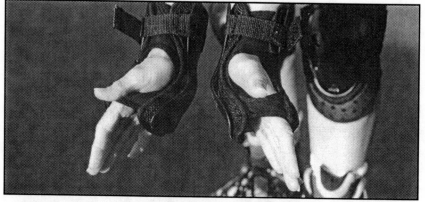

The click test—clap your hands and make sure you click.
A common mistake of beginners is wearing the guards
upside down or on the wrong hand.

Skates

After you get your skates laced, cinched or both, remember to adjust them after about ten to thirty minutes to make sure they are not too loose or too tight.

Wrist Guards

The majority of inline injuries are from falling on unprotected palms, snapping the wrists. Put on those wrist guards right now. Look at the picture to make sure they are not on the wrong hand, upside down, or both. You do not want to wave at your adoring public with your wrist guards in disarray.

Now it is time for you to rise and shine. To get up, flip to page 138, your guide to getting vertical.

Center Edge: Your feet should be shoulder width apart

Inside Edge: Your ankles lean inward and knees come together

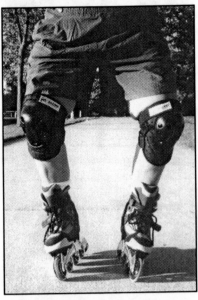

Outside Edge: Separate your feet and push your ankles outward

8

Beginning Moves for Babes who Groove

This chapter will teach you the basics used by beginners and experts. These will come in handy during your entire skating career.

EDGES FOR EDGY BABES

Your wheels have edges. Bet you didn't know that. There is the center edge, outside edge, inner edge, and corresponding edges. Pressure on particular edges during flight, err, skating, adds power to many marvelous moves you'll soon learn.

Stand on a surface where you will not roll, such as carpet or grass. This holds you securely and keeps you from taking off like a rocket. Put pressure on your different edges as indicated in the photos and get accustomed to how your skates feel when you apply pressure at different points. Edges are important because putting pressure on them while skating performs different functions, as you will learn when we get to the skills section.

Corresponding Edges

Corresponding Edges

With your feet about eight inches apart, push your right ankle inward and your left ankle outward. When you use these edges you will look like the cool Babe you were born to be, unless you accidentally skate into a solid object while you are doing it.

SAFE-T

Ground is not flat. It just looks that way. Once you are in skates, you will roll no matter how stinkin' flat the pavement appears. To stay put, stand in the Safe-T position. Place the heel of your non-braking skate against the inside arch of your other foot. Your brake foot is longer and a bit awkward, so try both and settle with what works best.

Center of Gravity

Some say a Babe's center of gravity is between her belly button and pelvic bone. What's important is that you are aware that you HAVE a center of gravity somewhere between your hips. Some skaters forget and try to balance with their skates and legs making them stiff. Others try to use their shoulders as the gravity center, making them top heavy. Remember, "my hips are my friends" in all things skating.

Ready Position

This position will save you from falling time and again. When your arms are flying around as if you're conducting an orchestra, immediately assume the ready position to regain balance.

1. Stand with your feet shoulder length apart.
2. Feet on center edge.
3. Looking forward with your back straight. Slightly bend your knees. From now on these are your shock absorbers. Do not bend at the waist—bend your knees.
4. Put your arms out in front of you in the "chipmunk position."
5. Your weight is over the balls of your feet, or the first two wheels of your skates.

Remember: If you straighten your back backwards, you'll fall that way.

Rotary Motion

Please understand that what you do with your upper or lower body influences your direction of travel. Sometimes this comes at unexpected moments. Rolling joyfully along in your neighborhood, you spy a neighbor and turn your upper body to cast a hearty wave. Oops, your act of pleasantry becomes an unexpected turn, surpris-

Your hips are your friends!

The Ready Position

ing both you and your neighbor. Try this:

- Stand on the grass or pristine, white carpet:
- Assume Ready Position—feet parallel, shoulder width apart.
- Turn your torso left, then right—keeping your hips facing forward.
- Turn your upper body, hips included, left then right.
- Turn hips only left, then right.
- You can turn your whole bod by aiming your upper body, or lower body, *towards* a target.
- These practices help beginners get used to moving their bodies while their feet remain stationary. The results will be very different when you try these on a paved surface.

MARIE CALLENDER® PIE

- Circle your left foot, with right foot remaining in position, in the shape of a half moon. Some Babes prefer to think of this shape as half of a Marie Callender ® pie. Your weight or "push" is on the inside edge of the arcing foot.
- Repeat with the other leg. Remember, your weight or "push" is on the inside edge.
- Really put your weight into the push. This gives it power and will eventually tighten your turns significantly.

Stances

Start in the ready position—knees bent, legs shoulder length apart, arms in front of you.

V-Stance—The Duck

Walk around on the lawn or carpet in this position. Start with your toes out, ankles in, just like a duck. Quacking is optional, mandatory if you are in public. You will learn to skate by "walking like a duck" in the V-stance. If you put your skates parallel, you will skate in place and go nowhere.

A-Stance

Stand with feet wider than your shoulders, which still carry the weight of the world on them. This A-Stance is a basic position when you turn. Your feet are on the inside edge.

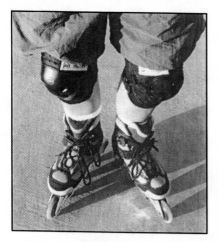

V-Stance

A-Stance

Scissor Stance

Scissor Stance

The back wheel of one skate is in front of the first wheel of the other. If it is hard to keep balance, shorten your scissor, and widen it (forward—not side to side) with practice. Shuffle back and forth as you glide. This builds balance used in stopping, turning, and looking like you know what you are doing.

9

Falling Like a Babe

Babes do not like to fall, but when it comes to inline skating, falling is foremost on our minds. You spend more energy thinking about it than the time it takes to happen—like getting a shot in your tender buns! Falls happen, so let's aim for a safe landing.

Many inline skating teachers perk up their students by falling on purpose and sliding ten feet during instruction. This is why we buy quality, adult safety gear. It stays on us when gravity strikes. Envision an ice skater falling. She slides on the ice and rarely gets injured. Your plastic safety gear acts as your "ice" when you visit the pavement.

Falling Like a Babe

- Quickly attempt to lean forward—in the Ready Position—when you feel the undeniable pull of gravity. That is where your gear is—in the front.
- Keep fingers up. You aren't a cat. Don't dig your claws into the ground.
- As you head towards the pavement, try to land first on your knees and then your wrist guards.
- Slide. This reduces the impact, significantly spreading it throughout your body instead of in just one place. Keep your chin up, eyes forward.

PRACTICE: Modified grass fall to practice falling.

♦ Get on carpet or grass.

♦ Carefully get down on your knees. You can't slide on turf like you can on pavement so *gently* get down on your knees and start there.

♦ Throw yourself forward, sliding your wrist guards across the grass. **Remember:** Fingers up.

♦ DO NOT CHEAT. Don't "walk" on your hands like a cat lowering itself to take a nap. Slide.

♦ Keep your head up. You don't want to till the soil with your nose.

Preventing Falls

Babes hate this. Sometimes we lose our balance or throw our arms out or back then fall backwards. Try to get your arms into the Ready Position the moment you feel off balance. If you lean back-

Problem: Lost Balance   Solution: Ready Position

WRONG: If you
don't get up the
right way, you may
skate in place.

wards while skating, you will head in the same direction—bottom first. If you feel unsteady, quickly bring your arms low in front of you and bend your knees. Glide for a moment or two until you feel stable. If you do fall backwards, you may find out why we recommend elbow guards. If you hit your rear end, this will hurt. Take stock for a moment and get up S-L-O-W-L-Y. Don't rush, although, if a commiserating crowd gathers around you, you will want to spring to your feet like nothing happened. No matter how capable one becomes on skates, falling can be embarrassing, but remember, you are a Babe. This will help you see the humor in what you just did, though it will probably be funnier later instead of sooner.

What Goes Down, Must Get Up

You will be seated when you put on your skates, or after a fall. Learn the proper way to rise with dignity.

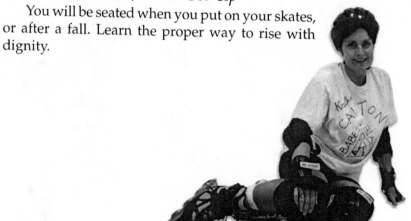

1. Roll over on your hands and knees like a Doberman.

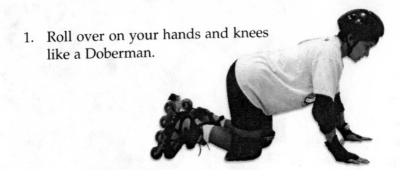

2. Get up on both knees like a chipmunk.

3. Put one knee up and grasp the top of your kneepad with your hands.

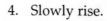

4. Slowly rise.
5. Put your feet in the Safe-T position and stand tall like you own the place. Smile.
6. You should try this procedure on the other leg and see which side works best for you.

Pat yourself on the back. Wait! Don't. It might make you lose your balance and sit back down.

Stroking pushes off. Striding rides the stroke.

10

Beginning Movement

Stroke, Stride, and Glide

Time to move, Babes. Get ready. Moving forward in the world of skating is called stroking, striding, and gliding. A stroke is the push that gets you moving forward and the glide is what your non-stroking leg does—it rolls. Striding consists of short strokes with toes pointed out like a duck. Beginners have shorter strokes and glides, which grow longer with experience.

Smokin' Strokin'

♦ Assume the Ready Position.

♦ Flex your ankles forward, knees bent.

♦ Silently tell yourself, "I can do this, I *can* do this."

♦ Look forward. Do not study your skates. It won't do you any good, as fascinating as they may be.

♦ Earlier, you walked like a duck on the grass or carpet. Walk like a duck from the grass onto pavement. Imagine doing the duck walk along a gigantic clock. Push off at 1:00 a.m. with your right leg and 11:00 p.m. with the left. Push one skate out from under you and slightly behind. Repeat with the other skate. Think Duck Stance. One o'clock, eleven o'clock, quack. One o'clock, eleven o'clock, quack. Start with

---

☞ Reminder ☜

· Put your weight on your right skate and *push*.
· Your left skate will move forward. Now put your weight over that skate keeping it directly under you as you glide forward.
· Return your right skate under you and push with the left.

---

small steps or glides. After you have skated across the playground four or five times, assume heartier, longer glides and push harder. Hold your glide and count "one, two" on one foot, then "one, two" on the other foot. Work up to "three, four." Start demure and strive for robust.

- Push your arms in front of you when you feel wobbly. If you accidentally throw your arms above or behind you, bring them forward to regain your balance.
- Combine stokes and glides.
- Hold the glide longer and longer—this strengthens your legs and increases your balance.

Striding Part II

⌒ Gliding Homework ↶

Glide on one foot for an extended period of time, and then the other foot. Keep your weight directly over your gliding foot. Count out loud "one-two" on one foot, then alternate. Practice and work up to the count of "five-six." The idea is to glide longer on one foot. This is your balance assignment. It will tighten your buns, force you to stabilize, and eventually help you conquer the world.

Gliding

Extreme Gliding

Now that you have striding under your belt (or fanny pack), try these next level skills:

- **Goal**: To stride longer and improve rolling balance.
- Increase intensity of glide and duration by holding the glide longer on each leg.
- Increase enthusiasm and self-confidence when you actually do this.

Stronger and Longer Stroke:

- To increase the intensity of the stroke you must push off harder and hold the glide longer with the opposite foot.
- Increase the bend in your knee. This lowers your center of gravity and puts more gusto in your push.
- Put more pressure on the inside edge of your skate when you push.
- Return your pushing leg under you, but don't put it down right away. This allows your glide leg, which is positioned directly under you, to roll longer.
- Increase the length of your stroke by counting "one, two, three, four…one, two, three, four, five…" and so forth.
- Glide with weight over gliding leg, which is positioned directly under you.
- Stay on gliding leg as long as you can. This builds muscle, strength, and balance.

☞ **Want Power?** ☜

- Stand tall and push off. Take notice of the length of your glide.
- Bend your knees and push. Notice your push has more power.

Combination of Stroke and Glide

- Combine the longer stroke and longer glide.
- Note the transition of one support leg to the other.
- Aim for continuous smooth movement as you push on one leg and then the other.

Swizzle

This is the move of moves. It will take you forward or backward and can be incorporated into advanced moves. When I encounter tricky spots on the skate trail, I sometimes swizzle. This enables me to keep all eight wheels on the ground. One can move fast or slow doing the swizzle. If you put some oomph into it, you can zip right along. This is also a great way to stop yourself (by tightening your legs mid-swizzle) if you roll unwillingly forward or backward.

♦ Assume V-Stance.

♦ Concentrate on your inside edges.

♦ Apply pressure and push yourself forward as if traveling along the shape of a series of connected footballs or hourglasses. You may wish to stroke and glide first and start swizzling from a moving position to get momentum.

♦ Your legs should go out shoulder width, or a little wider.

♦ At the widest part of your swizzle, point your knees inward and toes into an A-Stance (toes pointed inward) and then push out into a V-Stance (knees and toes outward).

♦ Imagine simultaneous leg arcs like you did with the Marie Callender Pie®.

♦ The deeper you bend your knees, the harder you will push.

♦ Knees/toes out. Knees/toes in. Repeat in one smooth movement.

♦ Try this while standing taller, and then "smaller" (knees bent deeply) and notice the difference.

♦ Do little swizzles and wider ones and compare.

♦ Don't swizzle too wide—just slightly wider than shoulder width at most.

♦ Apply pressure, propelling forward, linking each swizzle.

♦ This is great for tightening the inner thighs and rear end. Feel the pull. Feel the Babe within.

NOTE: Don't swizzle so wide that it looks like you are doing the splits on skates. Remember, don't push your feet much farther out than shoulder width.

Swizzle: Feet start in the "V" position.

Step 2: Push out and forward with oomph.

Step 3: Bring toes back in— repeat.

A

B

C

A: Glide in the Ready Position.

B: Turn your locked upper body.

C: Turn.

D: Turn.

E: Demand acknowledgement for a job well done.

D

E

11

Turning, Turning, Turning

Upper Body Turn or "A-Frame Turn"

Goal: This turn teaches you how to change directions, slow down, and "not go there."

Turning is one way to stop because it slows your momentum on a flat surface. If you don't turn quickly enough, you will stop. If you are going fast enough, you will turn. This constitutes two victories. Sometimes we don't want to go straight ahead, but don't want to stop or use the heel-brake to do so. Therefore, we embrace the turn!

Our upper bodies influence where the rest of us goes. You will notice without a doubt that turning works better in one direction than another. So practice on both sides, but don't be discouraged that one side "favors" another. This is normal. Do not take this as proof that you are normal. Babes don't see themselves as normal, but extraordinary.

- Find an object to skate around.
- Place a water bottle or your sweetie's cell phone on the ground to use as a "turning around point." A bright orange cone works, as does a box of truffles.
- Skate about fifteen to twenty feet away.
- Face the target and skate towards it with a look of determination on your face.
- Stride forward, then glide at the turning point.
- Assume Ready Position.
- Think of your body as one locked unit that moves together in unison with your upper body locked.
- Hold your arms straight out in front of you, as if clutching a

sterling silver tray with a latte on it. Turn your entire upper body to the left, and follow the tray. Stay stiff like Frankenstein's Monster. Do not spill your invisible coffee. It will stain your skates.

♦ Put weight on the inside edge of your right, outside skate and turn left. This will help whip you around. Remember, your outside leg influences the speed and power of the turn. If your outside leg is right, you turn left, if the outside leg is left, you turn right.

♦ Gads, this is a lot of explanations.

♦ Look at the pictures and do it.

☞ Hot Tips ☜

TIP: With turning in mind, do not reach to the right or left with your arms then just keep going straight. You want your whole body to follow your arms into a turn. Remember that your hands are locked to your wrists, which are locked to your elbows, which are locked to your shoulders, which are locked to your ribs, connected to your back. Move as a single unit. Make the rest of your body follow your hands and arms when you point left or right—turn the whole you left or right.

TIP: Your outside leg influences the speed and power of the turn. If your outside leg is right, you turn left, if the outside leg is left, you turn right.

My Hips Are My Friends or "Ride-the-Pie Turn"

Babes embrace their hips. Whether we like them or not, they are our friends in skating. They are not only our center of balance, they help us turn on a pie.

As before:

♦ Stride forward, then glide a moment.

♦ Assume Ready Position.

♦ Think of your body as one locked unit that moves together in unison, with your arms, upper body, waist, and hips.

♦ Approach the turning point.

- Pull your arms and the rest of you around the turning point.
- Picture a Marie Callender® Pie the size of an automobile tire. Ride half the pie with your outside skate putting pressure on the inside edge, squishing the pie and making a big mess. Do this with oomph. This will move you around much harder.
- Think about your hips and lower body as you push around the turn.

Parallel Turn

Think about the inside edge of outside skate, outside edge of inside skate

- Assume Ready Position.
- Scissor feet.
- Rotate your head and body towards the center of the turn.
- Pass the coffee tray by rotating the upper body into the turn.
- The inside leg is the support leg.
- Apply pressure to the outside edge of the inside skate.
- Apply pressure to the inside edge of the outside leg.

Do this several times in each direction. Once you feel comfortable turn to the right and immediately turn to the left and then back to the right. Use your waist and hips like a Babe and propel yourself right, left, right, left. Picture Marilyn Monroe walking in a hurry with high heels and a tight dress. Boomba boom ba boomba. Envision skiers coming down the hill swoosh, swoosh, swoosh. Now you are the swooshing, boomboom queen of the asphalt and your hips made it all possible. Pat them and thank them.

TRICKS TO BETTER TURNING

After you feel you can turn comfortably with confidence and balance try these techniques to put a punch in your turns. Try each one gently first, or the quick results may cause you to lose your balance, rolling into your skate mates and knocking the whole group down like colorful dominos with helmets.

Upper Body Turns:
- Point Turn
- Though it is not polite to point, Babes don't care.

♦ Glide forward.

♦ To turn right, point with your right hand in the direction you want to turn (right).

♦ Bring your left index finger/arm/shoulder blade/rib cage around to meet your outstretched right index finger.

♦ This pulls your upper body around.

Punch Turn

This whips your arms and shoulders around in the direction you want to go.

♦ Glide forward.

♦ Again, point to the right with your right hand.

♦ With your left arm, punch where you just pointed. Whoa. Not too hard or fast.

♦ This pulls your left shoulder, and you, around faster.

♦ Try not to punch yourself, Babe. That would be un-Babelike.

For added pleasure, imagine someone that has been mean to you and "punch" at him or her. You will be surprised what gusto this puts in your turn. It also gets old stuff out of our system that we don't need anyway. We call this Rolling Therapy.

Punch imaginary bad guys, not real ones because Babes shun police escorts, especially from the back seats of police cars. Though it has been established that some Babes grow weak in the kneepads at the site of a man in uniform.

With a little practice you'll be turning heads!
(photos by Suzan Davis)

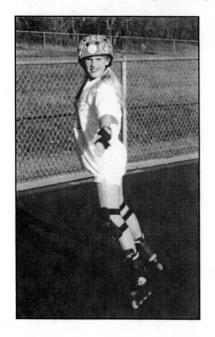

Bad choices in braking would include running into:

Car

Pole

Stop Sign

Bushes

Wall

Pavement

12

Stopping

Now that you can confidently go forward, it is a good time to discuss how to confidently stop going forward! Let me warn those who think they don't need this information: If you choose to skip your braking lesson, you will learn another kind of lesson—what your neighbor's lawn feels like at 25 miles per hour.

Do you think you can grab a flagpole at 15 mph and spin around and around like a tetherball until you come to a gentle stop? Your palms will be left on the pole and your landing gear will not be in position for a smooth descent.

Question: Why is the brake on the back?

A back brake can accommodate more weight then a front brake. You will need to use your body weight to stop. This works better than your face, though technically, both work.

The Heel Stop

First, practice on the grass or carpet. Stand in the Ready Position—hands forward, knees bent, a confident look on your face. Slide braking foot forward. Put that toe up. Good!

Make sure the fourth wheel of the brake (right) foot is near the first wheel of the support (left) foot. When you lift your toe, trans-

---

☞ Hot Tip☜

If you are "left-footed," you can move your brake to your left skate or have your dealer do it. Children's skates often come with brakes on both feet.

---

fer your weight to the heel of the braking leg. The more weight you push down on the heel, the faster you will stop. If you try to brake with your braking foot underneath you instead of scissored forward, you will knock yourself off balance.

Practice your technique any place where cars are not around, such as church parking lots, schoolyards on weekends, parking garages, and quiet cul-de-sacs—especially if the pavement is smooth.

Technique Using a Standard Brake

- Glide in Ready Position
- Your skates are a few inches apart, parallel and facing forward.
- Arms extended in front (chipmunk).
- Bend your knees.
- Lower center of gravity by doing a careful, slight squat. (Pretend you have buns of steel that weigh as much as buns of steel).
- Scissor your feet and move braking leg forward.
- The brake should be next to the front wheel of the nonbraking skate.
- Shift weight to nonbraking leg.
- Raise toe of braking foot.
- Shift weight to braking foot and press that pad into the asphalt.
- *STOP!*

This takes practice but is very effective. You can stop within 15 to 20 feet even if you are going over 20 mph.

ABT® Brake (Active Brake Technology)

ABT® brakes are cuff activated. When skaters with ABT® brakes scissor, the pressure of their extended calf will cause the brake to descend, stopping the skater before she puts up her toe. This technology takes out a step in skating—useful for beginners—but can accidentally "stop" an advanced skater dead in her tracks without warning. Experienced skaters adjust or dislodge the device in newer skates, using the ABT® brake like a standard model once their skills warrant this.

Gliding

Scissoring

Toe Up, heel down and put all your weight into the brake and STOP!

Remember that the last wheel of your braking leg is near the first wheel of your support or nonbraking leg.

ABT brakes are cuff activated   Standard heel brake

TIP: Start on a flat surface with no cars lurking around. Practice gliding in the scissor position. Do this on both legs so you won't overdevelop your braking leg compared to your supporting leg. We want you to remain the well-rounded individual you claim to be.

TIP: Don't try to stop on a dime (or any other piece of small change). Keep in mind you cannot stop on a dime, and be glad. If your brake could really do that, where would all that forward momentum take you? Your body would be at Aunt Beatrice's while your feet stayed at Uncle Weaver's—two houses down.

TIP: Look where you want to go. Do not study the ground or your toes.

TIP: It's okay to lean slightly forward if it helps you keep your balance, but remember your weight needs to be behind and slightly over the brake, not in front of it.

TIP: Resist lifting your toe before you have scissored far enough, or you can fall backwards, get off balance, or lose your leverage.

Legs too straight and
looking down, not forward

Leaning too far forward

Common Braking Boo Boo's

Not bending the knees enough
BAD: This can tip you backwards.
GOOD: Bending your knees lowers your Babe gravity center.

Leaning forward as if bowing
Bow if you must, but only *after* successfully braking, not during. Pause for applause.

BAD: When you lean forward you put your weight over or in front of your brake.

GOOD: You want your weight slightly behind the brake.

Not scissoring enough
BAD: If you do not scissor enough, you can fall forward.

GOOD: As you slide your braking foot forward, avoid lifting your toe too early. This engages the brake

Not scissoring enough

too early, making it difficult to keep your balance.

Throwing arms around as if you are conducting an orchestra

BAD: Babes like to throw their weight around, but this is not a good time.

GOOD: Remember to keep your arms in the Ready Position—chipmunk.

Not scissoring enough (close-up)

Throwing arms around throws your balance off. Don't forget your Ready Position!

**Legs too far apart turns you to the right.
Keep your weight slightly behind that brake!**

Having your legs too wide apart
Keep your legs together.
BAD: If your legs are spread apart too far, you can't apply as much pressure or weight on the brake.
GOOD: Squeeze those knees together like a little kid who needs to use the restroom. Scissor your braking foot forward. Remember, "my hips are my friends." Squeeze your knees, lower your hips, scissor and brake.

Benefits of the Heel Stop:
- ◆ You can perform high-speed stops.
- ◆ Both skates remain on the ground while stopping (though not all wheels of braking foot). This helps with balance.
- ◆ You can do it in tight places and narrow passageways around cars, bikes, and people.
- ◆ You can steer—point the toe of your braking foot where you want to go.
- ◆ The pad makes noise, alerting others of your presence.
- ◆ Brake pads are cheap to replace (about $6).

Leverage: This refers to stopping power and is influenced by the wear on your brake. A half-worn brake provides better leverage than a brand new one. At first your braking endeavors may feel

Practice builds confidence   Much better!
and competence.

awkward. Remember that if you are sporting new skates, the brake will need a "breaking-in period."

Tricks to Better Braking

Some folks resort to "tricks" that assist them to stop more fiercely and forcefully. The basic technique is always the same, but the mind focuses on particulars. These are the favorites of my students. Each one assists about twenty percent of the students. Take what works for you and leave the rest.

Soggy Diaper: Imagine a two-year-old with a very wet, sagging diaper. Picture how it droops, making his bottom look wide and low. Do the same. Push down on your right heel with your bottom wide and low.

Frustration Stop: Glide forward and when you stop clinch your fists and thrust your elbows downward. "Push" down with conviction. This can be renamed as the "Your-Cheating-Heart Stop," "I-Owe-More-Taxes-Than-I-Thought Stop," or "I-Locked-my-Keys-in-the-Car-with-Three-Bags-of-Groceries-in-the-Back-Seat Stop."

Aim-Straight Stop: Keep legs close together, move feet forward and apart in a scissor. If you stop with your legs far apart, you'll have less power and will probably veer to the right. To resolve this, tell your front wheel to head in a straight line. Steer it that way to counteract turning to the right. (People with their heel brakes on the left skate sometimes veer to the left.) It is very helpful to skate on the painted lines in empty school yards to hone our aim. We do not recommend using the line in the middle of the road.

Knees-Together Stop: Still scissoring your right skate, consciously try to keep your knees and thighs together. This puts more weight on your right heel. Take advantage of it, and stop like a Babe!

The Banana Slide: Pretend to squish a ripe, juicy banana with your heel, leaving a yellow trail of pulp about fifteen feet long. No banana bread for you Babe. Some Babes prefer to replace the banana with the image of an annoying co-worker. This enables them to stop with zest plus gets rid of stress, making these braking Babes more pleasant co-workers themselves.

Groovy Grass Stop

Grass is groovy because it is soft. Not the grass in my front yard of course, but certainly in my neighbor's. Let's practice there. Knowing how to do the grass stop is to know you have one more option in a life of fast choices.

+ Do not try this on raised sod or wet grass.
+ If the grass is thick or wet you will do a "hit and run" instead of a glide. Be ready because you will literally run on the grass with your skates feeling like lead boots. If you know this may be coming, you won't be caught off guard. Babes do not like to get caught off guard.
+ If you go too slowly, it won't work well. With practice, do this faster and faster for best results.

Grass Stop

+ Stroke and then glide in Ready Position.
+ Scissor the skate *nearest* the grass at least one skate length.
+ Roll onto the grass at an angle, keeping those arms forward and those buns low.
+ Never bend your back back; bend your knees and get low like an Eskimo.
+ You should roll, but it takes practice.

Scissor stance is most important in the grass stop.

Leg nearest to the grass extends forward. Bend the knees for stability.

Common Mistakes:

♦ *Not scissoring enough.* This makes you hit and hop or worse, soar like a flying squirrel, landing on your furry belly.

Remedy: Bend your knees and scissor as far as you can.

♦ *Scissoring with the wrong leg forward.* Many accidentally scissor the leg farthest from the grass instead of the leg which is closest to the grass.

Remedy: Make sure the skate next to the grass is the first to travel, well ahead of the follow-up skate.

♦ *Being thrust forward on impact.*

Remedy: You may be standing too straight. Bend deeply. The deeper the bend, the more stable you will be. Lower that backside. Lower your hips—your friends—as much as possible. Think of sitting down in a low chair, keeping your knees bent and your arms in the ready position.

Remember your forward swizzle? A backwards swizzle can stop you if you accidentally begin to roll backwards when you simply don't feel like it.

Skates too close together with weight too far forward...

...will throw you into the grass

Grass stop gone terribly wrong.

Snowplow

This stopping style is commonly used in skiing. It is basically a "mid-swizzle" stop. It requires more time to stop than using the heel brake but works nicely on flat surfaces and slight declines.

♦ Swizzle forward on a flat surface.

♦ At the widest point of the swizzle tighten the muscles in your legs, keeping your toes slightly in and your heels out.

♦ Put as much weight into your heels as possible and push down as hard as you can. Grind to a stop.

Backward Swizzle

Sometimes a skater will be chatting pleasantly with a neighbor and all of a sudden, start rolling backwards. It is a desperate feeling of being out of control. Take back control. Learn the backwards swizzle now.

Find a slight incline—not a hill, but a seemingly flat area where you actually roll slowly if you are not standing in the Safe-T position.

♦ Do one forward swizzle and stop midway by tightening your legs and holding your toes in, ankles out, pushing down.

♦ Retrace your path backwards. The moment you stop—success. The purpose is only to stop. Some skaters bring their feet back together under them into the Safe-T position. If this feels awkward, do another backwards swizzle. As soon as you stop, your mission is accomplished. It doesn't matter where your legs are under you as long as you feel stable and are no longer moving backwards on a downhill.

♦ Remember to stand in the Ready Position, arms forward, knees bent. This keeps you from falling backwards.

Students have found this a real confidence builder, giving them a feeling of control in an out-of-control world.

"Skating is something I can do with my kids."
Some claim that skating is a great way to wear out children.
However, things do not always go according to plan.

Stepping on or off a Curb

Up a Curb: The leg closest to the change of surface will go first.

Off a Curb: Same applies for going down

Stepping on or off a Rounded Curb

Rounded Curbs: Bend knees and scissor

13

Curb Your Enthusiasm

Curbs happen. Sometimes, when you least expect it, you face a quick decision upon curb approach: stop and step down or maintain speed and skate off as if it was a part of your schedule.

Skating up a Curb

Scenario: A street meets a sidewalk at a curb.

Approach curb.

1. Shift weight to back leg.
2. Step above curb and set front foot down.
3. Shift weight to upper foot.
4. Lift back foot onto curb.

Skating Off a Curb

Scenario: Sidewalk with curb leading to street.

1. Maintain comfortable speed.

Roll up or down in one smooth, continuous motion

2. Approach curb with all eight wheels on the ground and scissor.
3. Skate off curb maintaining scissor stance.
4. Upon touchdown, use your shock absorbers—your knees and ankles—to bend slightly forward to absorb the shock.

Rounded Curbs

Many neighborhoods feature rounded curbs. You can roll up or down these without lifting up and down, thus keeping all wheels on the ground.

1. Roll towards curb at an angle.
2. Remember that you are fearless.
3. If curb is on your left side, scissor your left leg forward and roll up or down the curb in one smooth and solid motion.
4. If curb is on your right side, scissor your right leg forward and roll up or down the curb.
5. Remember to bend your knees to maintain balance and that your knees are your shock absorbers.
6. Keep your weight on the back part of the skate, not the front.
7. Roll with it, Baby.

Remember to scissor on approach and descent

Bend those knees! Let them absorb the shock.

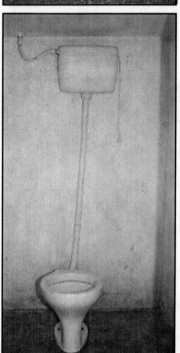

Oh, oh, the places you'll go...

14

Special Skills for Babes in Need

The Potty Stop

GOAL: Use public restrooms without rolling out the door with your pants down giving the innocent public a full moon at high noon. This is one of those skills most Babes learn by "hit and miss"—mostly miss. This is your chance to learn it correctly.

This works in public restrooms and port-a-potties. Many Babes initially snort that they will *never* use one of those. You will. When the weight of your fanny pack feels like a sack of rocks on your bladder, you will experience "willingness over fear." Hint: Do not entertain taking off your skates. Many public restrooms have wet floors and it is not from rain.

Practice on a couch or bench, skipping bullet point number four.

Take off and Landing: Reverse Order

LANDING:

♦ Approach toilet and proclaim, "You will not conquer me."

♦ Turn your back seat to the toilet seat and touch the porcelain with the back of your leg. Hopefully, it will be dry.

♦ Put your toes together so you won't roll, or place toe of right skate on end, keeping your first wheel on the ground, lifting all others.

♦ Pull down your pants.

♦ Go down low and slow.

♦ Use your imagination.

TAKE OFF

♦ Place toe of right skate on end, keeping your first wheel on the ground, lifting all others.

You won't conquer me!

- Push up from this wheel and stand, keeping knees slightly bent for balance.
- Remember, if the port-a-pot is on a grade, you will roll into the door, so do not point your skates towards the door but in an "A" (toes pointed inward) or at an angle.
- Another option is to put your braking foot forward and press down on your heel, employing your brake, and lifting up. Put your weight on the brake as you rise.
- Pull yourself together.
- Congratulate your Babe self and exit with a look of victory instead of a gaze of bladder urgency.

A little privacy, please

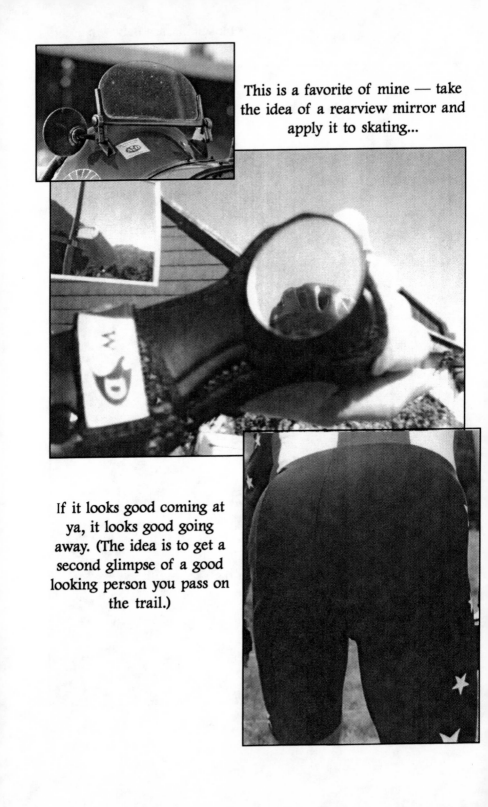

This is a favorite of mine — take the idea of a rearview mirror and apply it to skating...

If it looks good coming at ya, it looks good going away. (The idea is to get a second glimpse of a good looking person you pass on the trail.)

15

Special Equipment

"Babe-Wear"

Babes come equipped. A "must have" product is a mirrored wrist guard. Go to a sporting goods or art/crafts store that sells good quality round mirrors. Those two or three inches in diameter work well. Velcro® it to the back of your left wrist guard. When you want to know what is behind you, lift your hand and look in the mirror. This enables you to check for traffic without turning your head, which takes your eyes off the road ahead for too long. In an instant you can access the situation behind you.

Bike mirrors that attach to helmets work well, but many Babes find the vibrations of skating makes it look like you are viewing the contents of a whirling blender. Unfortunately, this Babe used to get distracted by her ever-present helmet mirror, then look into it and skate into potholes. I now prefer mirrors that are handy and on the back of my hand.

Added Benefits

Babe-Wear Bonus

"If it looks good coming at you, it looks better going away."

If a He-Babe approaches and then passes in the opposite direction, the party is *not* over. Life's pleasures come in brief moments. Maximize this one and look into your wrist-guard mirror to get a gander at his backside. If it is wrapped in tight material, perched on a bike seat, you won't be sorry. A sly Babe can surreptitiously stare without being seen by polite society. Such moments of beauty will inflame your passion for inline skating. You will be surprised at how often you'll use this technique when weekend workout warriors head for the public pathways.

Ready...

Aim...

Fire!

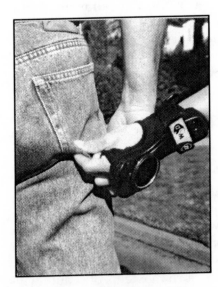

A firm pinch takes skill
and practice

If you are fast enough, you
will be gone before he knows
what hit him.

16

Tricks for Tacky Babes

Not all Babes strive for good behavior. This shocking revelation is a surprise to many, but not to Babes. Try these skills at your own risk and only on other Babes, or you will find yourself in trouble, which may be your goal in the first place.

SKATE-BY CRIMES OF PASSION

(For best attacks, approach from the back)

Skate-by Poking

Many parks have pathways shared by both skaters and pedestrians. Babes always look out for people and treat them with respect. They try not to sneak up on them and say "Boo!" when they pass because this gives skaters a bad name, though it sometimes gives Babes great pleasure.

As a side note, never try "skate-bys" on men walking dogs. If you hear "sic 'em," skate like hell.

At times, we have to put good manners aside in emergency situations. If you see a male you cannot resist, but are too shy to stop for a chat or propose marriage on the spot, some playful Babes compromise. Carefully study the height of his hips compared to the length of your arm. Skate by carefully, as you don't want to knock him over, plus you want a clean getaway. As you glide casually past, reach behind him and poke him in the ribs or in the behind. Act as if nothing happened and glide away. If you have a Babe mirror on your wrist guard, check for his reaction, but do not turn around. This implicates your guilt. You are not guilty of anything but being a Babe. Your actions are inconsequential to your Babe label, which gives you special rights that no one can take away.

Sometimes getting caught isn't all bad after all.

Skate-by Pinching

It takes practice to pull off a skate-by pinching because you have to stop and take off again. It is hard to grip a man's denim-covered rump between your forefinger and thumb while traveling at thirteen miles per hour. Settle for a friendly poke. Not recommended if the man is on a bicycle. He will track you down and you will be forced to face the music.

Skate-by Hatting

Same principles apply. This time, however, know you may actually make the person really mad. Have your hand out several seconds before you approach and gingerly lift the hat up and off the victim, clutch the article and maintain your sliding stroke. With practice, it will become one smooth, continuous motion from hat extraction to pumping your arms for a graceful gliding getaway. Hat lifting messes up hair and exposes bald spots, so do not expect applause, though miraculously, some men find this amusing and get their hopes up that this is a signal that you will have sex with them.

A back approach is
always best.

Snatch hat and flee.
A victory squeal
makes for more fun.

Skate like heck or
tease your victim if
he seems friendly.

179

Babes who stretch together... kvetch together?

17

Stretching

Warming up and Cooling Down

Some folks ask about stretching before skating. Never stretch cold muscles. Most Babes skate slowly, gliding easily for five to ten minutes to warm muscles before strenuous skating and mischief. Some skaters stretch after their adventure on skates.

After-Skate Stretching

When you are ready to call it a day, give your body time to cool off by skating at an easy pace for five or ten minutes. Then kick off your skates and stretch on a nice soft, dog-doodle-free area of grass. Since you are already sitting down, let's start there.

Remember to move slowly. Stretch until you feel a slight pull. This pull feeling should diminish as you hold the position. If it doesn't, ease up. Remember, stay comfortable. You are a Babe and Babes love comfort, among other things.

(Text and models for drawings courtesy of *Stretching 20th Anniversary Revised Edition®* by Robert A. Anderson and Jean E. Anderson.)

Stretching should be done slowly without bouncing. Stretch to where you feel a slight, easy stretch. Hold this feeling for 5-30 seconds. As you hold this stretch, the feeling of tension should diminish. If it does not, just ease off slightly into a more comfortable stretch. The easy stretch reduces tension and readies the tissues for the developmental stretch.

After holding the easy stretch, move a fraction of an inch farther into the stretch until you feel mild tension again. This is the developmental stretch, which should be held for 5-30 seconds. This feeling of stretch tension should also slightly diminish or stay the same.

If the tension increases or becomes painful, you are over-stretching. Ease off a bit to a comfortable stretch. The developmental stretch reduces tension and will safely increase flexibility.

Hold only stretch tensions that feel good to you. The key to stretching is to be relaxed while you concentrate on the area being stretched. Your breathing should be slow, deep, and rhythmical. Do not worry about how far you can stretch. Stretch relaxed and limberness will become just one of the many by-products of regular stretching.

*Note: if you have had any recent surgery, muscle or joint problem, please consult your personal health care professional before starting a stretching or exercise program.

ARMS AND SHOULDERS

Overhead stretch: Interlace your fingers above your head. Now, with your palms facing upward, push your arms slightly back and up. Feel the stretch in your arms, shoulders and upper back. Hold stretch for 15 seconds. Do not hold your breath. This stretch is good to do anywhere, anytime.

Shoulder Shrug: Raise the top of your shoulders toward your ears until you feel slight tension in your neck and shoulders. Hold this feeling of tension for 3-5 seconds, and then relax your shoulders downward into their normal position. Do this 2-3 times. Good to use at the first signs of tightness or tension in the shoulder and neck area.

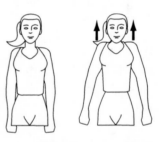

One Arm Stretch: Hold your left arm just above the elbow with your right hand. Now gently pull elbow toward opposite shoulder as you look over your left shoulder. Hold stretch for 15-20 seconds. Do both sides.

Double Arm Stretch: The next stretch is done with your fingers interlaced behind your back. Slowly turn your elbows inward while straightening your arms. This stretch can be done at any time. Hold for 5-15 seconds. Do twice.

Elbow Stretch: With arms overhead, hold the elbow of one arm with the hand of the other arm. Keeping knees slightly bent (1 inch), gently pull your elbow behind your head as you bend from your hips to the side. Hold an easy stretch for 10 seconds. Do both sides. *Keeping your knees slightly bent will give you better balance.*

LEGS AND HIPS

Calf Stretch: To stretch your calf, stand a little way from a solid support and lean on it with your fore-arms, your head resting on your hands. Bend one leg and place your foot on the ground in front of you leaving the other leg straight, behind you. Slowly move your hips forward until you feel a stretch in the calf of your straight leg. Be sure to keep the heel of the foot of the straight leg on the ground and *your toes pointed straight ahead.* Hold an easy stretch for 15-20 seconds. Do not bounce. Stretch both legs.

Opposite Hand to Opposite Foot Stretch (quads and knee stretch): Hold top of left foot (from inside of foot) with right hand and gently pull heel moving toward buttocks. Hold for 15-20 seconds. Do both legs.

Relax Hamstings: Stand in this bent-knee position which contracts the quadriceps and relaxes the hamstrings. Hold for 30 seconds.

Because these muscles have opposing actions, tightening the quadriceps will relax the hamstrings. As you hold this bent-knee position, feel the difference between the front of the thigh and the back of the thigh. The quadriceps should feel hard and tight while the hamstrings should feel soft and relaxed.

Frog Stretch: With your feet shoulder width apart and pointed out to about a 15-degree angle with heels on the ground, bend your knees and squat down. If you have trouble staying in this position hold onto something for support. It is a great stretch for your ankles, Achilles tendons, groin, lower back, and hips. Hold stretch for 10-20 seconds. *Be careful if you have had any knee problems. If pain is present, discontinue this stretch.*

Kneel Stretch: As shown in the drawing, move one leg *forward until the knee of the forward leg is directly over the ankle.* Your other knee should be resting on the floor. Now, without changing the position of the knee on the floor or the forward foot, lower the front of your hip downward to create an easy stretch. This stretch should be felt in front of the hip and possibly in your hamstrings and groin. This will help relieve tension in the lower back. Hold the stretch for 15-20 seconds.

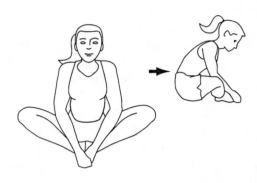

Butterfly Stretch: Put the soles of your feet together with your heels a comfortable distance from your groin. Now, put your hands around your feet and slowly contract your abdominals to assist you in flexing forward until you feel an easy stretch in the groin. Make your movement forward by bending *from the hips* and not from the shoulders. If possible, keep your elbows on the outside of your lower legs for greater stability during the stretch. Hold a comfortable stretch for 20-30 seconds.

Trunk Twist: Sit with your right leg straight. Bend your left leg, cross your left foot over and rest it on the outside of your right knee. Bend your right elbow and rest it on the outside of your upper left thigh, just above the knee. During the stretch, use your elbow to keep this leg stationary with controlled pressure to the inside. Now, with your left hand resting behind you, slowly turn your head to look over your left shoulder, and at the same time rotate your upper body toward your left hand and arm. As you turn your upper body, think of

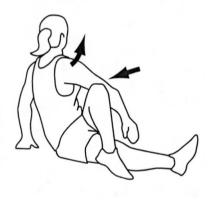

turning your hips in the same direction (though your hips will not move because your right elbow is keeping the left leg stationary). This should give you a stretch in your lower back and side of hip. Hold for 15 seconds. Do both sides. Don't hold your breath; breathe easily.

Straddle Stretch: Next, straighten your left leg. The sole of your right foot will be resting next to the inside of your straightened leg. Lean slightly forward *from the hips* and stretch the hamstrings of your left leg. Find an easy stretch and relax. If you can't touch your toes comfortably, use a towel to help you stretch. Hold for 15-20 seconds. Do not lock your knee. Your left quadriceps should be soft and relaxed during the stretch. Keep your left foot upright with the ankle and toes relaxed. Do both legs. Do not hold your breath.

NECK AND BACK

Stretch diagonally: Point the toes of your

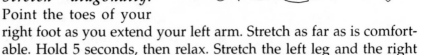

right foot as you extend your left arm. Stretch as far as is comfortable. Hold 5 seconds, then relax. Stretch the left leg and the right arm the same way.

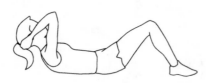

Sit-up Stretch: Interlace your fingers behind your head and rest your arms on the floor or grass. Using the power of your arms, <u>slowly</u> bring your head, neck and shoulders forward until you feel a slight stretch. Hold an easy stretch for 5 seconds. Repeat three times. Do not overstretch.

Hamstring Stretch: Next, straighten both legs and relax, then pull your right leg toward your chest. For this stretch keep the back of your head on the floor or grass, if possible, but do not strain. Hold an easy stretch for 30 seconds. Repeat, pulling your left leg toward your chest.

Twist Stretch: From a bent-knee position, interlace your fingers behind your head and lift the left leg over the right leg. From here, use your left leg to pull your right leg toward the floor until you feel a stretch along the side of your hip and lower back. Stretch and relax. Keep upper back, shoulders and elbows flat on the floor. The idea is not to touch the floor (or grass) with your right knee, but to stretch within <u>your</u> limits. Repeat for the other leg.

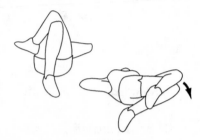

Important Things to Remember when Stretching:

- Do not stretch too far.
- Hold the stretch comfortably.
- Breathe slowly and deeply but naturally. Never hold your breath.
- Never bounce. This tightens the very muscles you are trying to stretch. Stretch and hold.
- Think about the area you are stretching and the low-fat frozen yogurt you'll have when you get home.
- Don't *try* to be flexible. That will come in time as a result of proper stretching.

Remember Babes like to stretch. Sometimes they stretch themselves; sometimes they stretch the truth. But certainly, a Babe on Blades will stretch her world.

Sample Journal page

The hardest thing I did on skates today:

What I learned:

Improved over last time:

How I feel about it:

My next goal on skates:

How it affected my home life:

How it affected my working life:

How it affected my life in general:

How my quest to take a risk empowered me on the home front:

How it affects my working life:

How it affects my thinking and confidence:

How it affects my life and Babehood in general

Things I have put off for ages:

I will accomplish one of these untackled tasks tomorrow or let it go forever.

18

Babe Journaling

Journal writing is a craze these days and one can even take classes in it at numerous colleges. An "Idiots Guide to Journal Writing" is lurking near you at a local bookstore. Babes like to keep things simpler than reading a whole book on how to keep things simple. They do, however, recognize that a billion people can't be wrong and there are definite benefits to keeping a journal. It is a part of your road to ultimate Babe empowerment.

Writing thoughts in a journal helps us get "out of our own way." What comes out of the pen often surprises us, providing insight to the Babe writer. Babes enjoy keeping a journal at first, especially before, during, and after taking lessons. Making journal notations on a weekly basis, or after learning to skate, serves us well. Upon reflecting back on The Babe Journal, you discover just how far you have come. You otherwise may forget how scared you were of the mountain down the road that magically, in time, becomes a speed bump. (Which it was in the first place.)

Journals also allow us to see how much we change as our physical confidence increases and the effect that has on our day-to-day lives. Our minds are busy and our memories are short (sometimes on purpose). Keeping track of with whom we skate, where, and our thoughts at the time makes for great reading later. Trust me. It is too easy to ignore the progress we make in life unless we have documentation. Do it. Keep a Babe Journal. You can call it a Fear/Slash/Victory Journal. It will help you keep track of the mental and spiritual advantages of trying something new. It is one more way to help you become the radiant Babe you are born to be.

Babes can get wild with their skate clubs.

19

Start Your Own Club

Start a Babe Franchise

You will not make a bundle, which is hard to do with clubs, but you can cover expenses and make a few bucks while meeting an incredible assortment of like-minded people.

What you will need:

Babes. Sadly, many women—and men—are not aware that they are Babes. They are, and it is *your* mission to show them how to reclaim their Babe within. This allows males to resurface their inner children and women to reclaim their inner goddesses.

A Consistent Schedule. Choose a meeting place that is flat and free of traffic. Contact the local paper by phone and then fax/e-mail so a notice can be placed in the calendar or events section of the paper. It must be at the same place at the same time *every week* for best results.

Babe Franchise. Cost: $195. You will receive:

♦ Ten iron-on transfers of Babes on Blades log for members to place on their favorite T-shirts. The logo not only identifies individuals as Babes, but serves as a warning (or promise) to the rest of the populace.

♦ Personalized autographed book for the club president.

♦ Additional autographed Babe Books to resell to your club. You will receive a savings of $20.00 for five books, $40.00 for ten, $80.00 for twenty — or $4.00 per book on orders of ten books or more. State sales tax and shipping still apply.

♦ Sample press releases for your events.

♦ Sample flyers.

♦ The feeling that today you are taking over the neighborhood, tomorrow, the universe. Babe memberships typically cost $25 to $35 (more if you include a book) so you can make back your money, plus have some left over for coffee and dessert.

To start a club, cheerfully send your check to Babes on Blades, P.O. Box 699, Roseville, CA 95678. Include your name, mailing address, e-mail, and phone number. Write neatly or type this information, as the Babe staff is unable to decipher scribble, though we are keen at Scrabble.

www.babesonblades.org

The National Skate Patrol teaches
braking techniques on the spot.

Appendix A: IISA

THE INTERNATIONAL INLINE SKATING ASSOCIATION (IISA)

INTERNATIONAL IN-LINE SKATING ASSOCIATION

This outstanding organization works round the clock so Babes and those they cherish can skate as safely as possible in as many places as possible. Without this organization, many locales we now enjoy would be illegal to skaters.

Throughout the United States, legislation is introduced on a regular basis to ban inline skating in parks and other venues because someone has asked his or her legislator to support a bill or amendment banning inline skating from public areas. The IISA helps legislators and others understand that skating is enjoyed for sport, fitness and vitality by responsible adults, not just by reckless members of society who have lots of time and no responsibilities.

I once asked an elected official why Patricia Musselman, a sixty-eight-year-old Babe on Blades, could not skate in his district. She had paid taxes longer than many of us, and these taxes were used to build the paths that others enjoy for cycling, jogging, pushing strollers and walking dogs. I showed him a photograph of about fifty Babe members, all posing with their helmets, safety gear and colorful Babe shirts, all taxpayers, the majority over forty years old.

"What is it about Pat and these people that makes you want to ban them?" I asked.

His answer, "Good question, I never thought of it like that. I envisioned skaters as reckless and irresponsible."

The IISA and its volunteers work hard to educate legislators like the one above. Thanks to this effort, we are free to skate in many locations that would be illegal otherwise.

In 1995, Captain John Butterfield, formerly of the IISA, told me to get Babes to wear helmets and take a lesson so they would have a good skating experience. This was not easy because there were few instructors available. The training and ability of area inline skating teachers seemed questionable when instructors showed up at lessons with no helmet or safety equipment. The IISA has remedied this problem with their Inline Certification Program (ICP). Find a certified instructor in your area by checking out www.iisa.org.

Also on IISA's web page, you will discover a wealth of information from how to buy your first pair of skates to statistics and news regarding the sport. This expansive site also provides skate links and a long list of useful resources.

The following material is courtesy of www.iisa.org. It tells about the organization and their programs.

> The International Inline Skating Association (IISA) is a non-profit trade organization that works to advance the sport of inline skating. The organization was founded in 1991 by a group of manufacturers, retailers and skaters who chose to be proactive about enhancing the future of the sport. Since then, the IISA has developed effective educational programs promoting safe skating, plus has protected and expanded access to public skate ways across the country.

The IISA headquarters are located in Wilmington, NC. In addition to this office, a nationwide network of volunteers work with local governments to maintain skate access and ensure good civic relations through the Government Relations and National Skate Patrol (NSP) programs.

The IISA Inline Certification Program (ICP) is a professional teaching program that certifies people to become inline skating instructors. The IISA/ICP is recognized worldwide as the premier certification program for inline skating and conducts programs in Canada, Europe, Japan and Southeast Asia.

Inline Certification Program (ICP)

The Inline Certification Program (ICP) is devoted to the development of professional inline skating instructors whose purpose is educating the public by the safest, most effective skill-building methods available. Through certified instructors, the ICP provides a consistent educational framework for skaters around the world.

How the Program Works: Each year, the Inline Certification Program creates national and international test sites and conducts community-based clinics for inline skaters who want to become certified inline instructors. National examiners who have demonstrated superior ability as skaters and instructors conduct clinics. ICP clinics use a consistent, comprehensive and tested program for inline instruction, based on a standardized format of teaching progressions and terminology. Once certified, skaters join a growing organization of inline instructors who bring a skill building approach to educating inline skaters throughout the world.

Certification is generally a weekend program. The clinic includes classroom work, a teaching seminar held on skates, a written test and a practical exam in which instructors are scored while teaching a class. In addition, round table discussions on skate bans, safety issues and getting started occur throughout the weekend.

ICP Certified Instructors are educated and examined by a panel of highly skilled professionals. ICP Examiners have extensive inline skating experience as well as educational and technical knowledge. Examiners also have athletic and coaching backgrounds in related sports and have successfully completed the ICP Apprentice Examiner Program (AEP). This elite group develops ICP teaching methodology and runs certification programs.

Certified instructors receive liability insurance for inline instruction. Local ICP continuing education seminars and workshops reinforce teaching skills. The annual ICP Inline Expo provides an opportunity for product testing, skill clinics and the exchange of information from other instructors. A quarterly newsletter keeps ICP instructors informed on significant product developments, event dates, national inline news, new teaching methods and better ways to organize and promote classes.

Levels of Certification. There are currently three levels of certification:

Level 1 Certification is for the entry-level instructor who wants to teach the fundamentals of inline skating based on a standardized format of teaching. Instructors are qualified to teach such things as moving, stopping and turning.

Level 2 Certification is for the experienced Level 1 Instructor who wishes to enhance class-handling skills, problem solving and intermediate-level skill development. Level 2 Instructors teach skills such as backward movement, alternative stopping, crossovers and street-skating awareness.

Master Certification (formerly Level 3) includes certifications in high skill areas such as Fitness, Racing, Freestyle, and Street skating. Prior specialty experience is recommended before attending these certification courses, but Master Certification is open to all current Level 1 instructors.

The National Skate Patrol

The National Skate Patrol (NSP) is a network of proficient volunteers who help skaters to better coexist with cyclists, pedestrians and other park and trail users. These red-shirted volunteers conduct free braking clinics, offer tips on skate etiquette, and otherwise assist new and experienced skaters alike. The New York Skaters Association (NYRSA) and IISA developed the National Skate Patrol in 1992.

The mission of the National Skate Patrol (NSP) is to provide a service to skaters using public skate ways, be they parks, trails, or roads. NSP volunteers provide free on-the-spot stopping instruction to skaters having difficulty skating under control. In addition, they distribute skate safety maps and work with the local police, parks departments, and skate retailers. Many are Certified Instructors and all encourage skaters to follow the Rules of the Road.

Government Relations

The Government Relations Program (GRP) protects environments where skating can be safely practiced.

Inline Advocacy. The Government Relations Program maintains a comprehensive database of information relating to inline skating restrictions. In addition, the committee provides a forum for dialog among governmental officials, retailers and skaters. They also provide consultation and expert testimony in matters relating to inline skating. Over 1,000 volunteers have either worked with the Government Relations Program or have provided aid in opposing restrictions.

Legislative Monitoring. The Government Relations Program effort monitors legislative initiatives on a weekly basis. New legislation, the status on proposed bills, amendments and committee hearings are tracked.

Highlights of Activities. Since 1991, the Government Relations Program has successfully defended skating venues in more than three dozen locations, including Central Park, New York City; Venice Beach, California; Rochester, Michigan; Palm Beach, Florida; Birmingham, Alabama; Portland, Oregon and London, Ontario, Canada. These efforts and the continuing work of the Government Relations Program help to substantiate the right to skate.

Helmets and Protective Gear. The IISA supports legislation that requires children eighteen and under to wear helmets. The Association strongly encourages *all* participants, regardless of age or level of expertise, to wear helmets that meet the standards of recognized organizations including ANSI, Snell, ASTM, and HECC.

Volunteers. The volunteer group is comprised of individuals from sponsoring corporations, skate clubs, retailers, media, parks and recreation departments and municipalities. Committee members spearhead special projects, monitor skating restrictions, assist individuals with specific concerns and foster the development of new skating venues.

Appendix B: Glorious Glossary

Coming to Terms with Terms

ABEC

Acronym standing for Annular Bearing Engineering Council. ABEC ratings correlate to the speed of the bearing with lower ABEC ratings spinning at slower speeds than higher ABEC ratings. The ABEC-1, ABEC-3, ABEC-5, and ABEC-7 ratings indicate that the bearings meet the stated ABEC prescription for particular precision levels.

ABT Braking System

Braking method using a special mechanism mounted on the back of the skate cuff which presses the brake pad downward when the skater scissors into braking position. The back of one's calf puts pressure on the boot cuff that engages the brake. All four wheels never leave the ground as with the heel stop. Sometimes referred to as Cuff-Activated Braking System.

A-Frame

A wide stance used to start turning movements. Also called the Frankenstein turn. Helps create balance and a low center of gravity.

Action Leg

Leg opposite the support leg. It performs the "action" part of the skill.

Aggressive

Style of skating using skates with small flat wheels which help participants flip upside down and backwards, glide down stairs and handrails, off park benches and curbs, and other objects close to *No Rollerblading* signs. The emphasis is on stunts.

Allen wrench
Tool used to unscrew the bolts that hold the wheels and brake. Most new skates include one in the box. It is an L-shaped hexagonal metal bar either end of which fits the socket of a screw or bolt. Invented by the Allen Manufacturing Company in 1943. (Good inline skate trivia question.)

ANSI
American National Standards Institute. Establishes protective equipment standards. ANSI-certified means that the gear complies with certain design specifications for safety. ANSI-certified helmets and gear usually have a sticker inside the product denoting this.

ASTM
American Standards for Testing Materials. Establishes protective equipment standards. ASTM-certified means that the gear complies with certain design specs for safety.

Anti Rocker
A wheel configuration used by many rail-sliders where the larger wheel is on the toe and heel, and smaller wheels are in the middle, in position two and three. This allows one to slide down handrails without the wheels getting in the way. Most Babes do not rocker their skates. But some do. One cannot predict what a Babe will do, time and time again.

Babe
YOU

Babe Gear
Specific products or equipment with special enhancements to make them "Babe friendly" such as mirrored wrist guard.

Bearings
Mounted in pairs inside the hub of each wheel, they reduce friction and allow the wheels to spin smoothly.

Bearing Spacers
Plastic or metal parts that go in between the bearings so the axles can go through the wheels.

Blur
Unbelievably fast Babe.

Boot
The part of the skate that holds your tender foot.

Brake
The rubber stop most often found on the right skate. Can be round or square.

Braking Leg
Not as bad as it sounds. It is the leg performing the stopping movement.

Center edge
When skates are perpendicular to the asphalt, this part touches the ground.

Center of gravity
The distribution of weight that keeps you balanced evenly. It is central in not falling. The lower the center of gravity, the more balance a skater will have. It lies between your pelvis and belly button.

Chassis
Part of a skate that holds the frame in place, also called the frame.

Corresponding edges
Both skates are angled in the same direction with one skate on its outside edge and the other on its inside edge.

Crossover
Move that crosses the outer skate over the inside skate. Allows one to turn and maintain speed simultaneously. An advanced technique used mostly by speed skaters. Looks cool until you fall on your face.

Cuff
The part of the skate that encases the ankle, often made of stiff material.

Cuff-Activated Braking System
Braking method that uses a special mechanism mounted on the back of the skate cuff that presses the brake pad downward when

the skater scissors foot forward. The back of the calf puts pressure on the boot cuff that engages the brake. All four wheels never leave the ground, unlike the heel stop. Sometimes referred to ABT braking system.

Diameter

The size of a skate wheel measured through the center in millimeters (mm). Larger wheels roll you faster than small ones.

Duck walk

Just like it sounds, walking with your skates turned in at the heels and out at the toes in the shape of a "V". Good for beginners to practice on the grass to get used to the feel of skating.

Durometer

A measure of the hardness of polyurethane wheels. The higher the durometer, the harder the wheel.

Edge

Portion of wheel in contact with the pavement. Skate wheels have three edges – the center, inner, and outer. These factor in turns and numerous maneuvers. Different skills are performed on different edges.

Frame

The part of the skate under the boot that holds the wheels in place. Also called chassis.

Frame Spacer

Small parts that go between wheels and the runners.

Fitness/Cross Training

Similar to recreational skates, they are often lighter with a low-cut boot and larger wheels. Used by those out to burn calories and skate long distances to get in shape.

Freestyle

Type of inline skating most similar to ice figure skating, also called artistic.

Glide

When the skate rolls after a stroke.

Grass stop

Also called bailout. When skater heads for a grassy area to avoid trouble, slow down, or stop.

Grind

To slide along a rail or edge of object using a skate surface other than the wheels.

Grind plate

Metal or plastic piece on skate frame that helps someone younger than you or me slide or *grind* along a park bench, handrail, or some other forbidden object.

Half-pipe

A U-shaped ramp used by aggressive skaters.

He-Babe

A male skater who possesses the right qualifications as determined by a Babe. Also, a man who supports his skating wife or girlfriend with such enthusiasm, he earns the title by his tireless service and contribution to her happiness, even if he does not skate.

Heel Stop

Stopping method using the heel brake.

Helmet

Please tell me you know what this is. Also known as Brain Bucket, prevents disaster to irreplaceable parts. Helmets should be ASTM, ANSI or Snell-approved.

Hop-Up Kits

An upgrade kit that includes frame spacers, bearing spacers, and axles. Hop-up kits allow folks to whack down on their skates with gusto without compressing or cracking the spacers. Mostly used by aggressive skaters.

Hub

The hard substance to which the polyurethane of the wheel is bonded. Bearings fit in the hub of the wheel.

Inline

Proper name for inline skates and the sport of inline skating. The wheels are in a line. Some folks think it refers to skaters rolling in a line. It is almost impossible for Babes to roll in a straight line, as they enjoy swerving, seemingly out of control, on a regular basis. They also embrace the element of surprise.

Inside Edge
The side of the wheel facing inward.

Inside Skate
The skate that makes the smaller arc during a turn.

Liner
The inner skate boot or cushion.

Outside Edge
Side of wheel facing out.

Outside Skate
During a turn, this skate creates the larger arc radius.

Parallel Turn
When skates move side by side and skater uses corresponding edges to turn.

Power slide (backward)
Braking method used during high speeds going backwards by people younger and faster than I. The left leg is the support and the right leg is the braking leg.

Profile
Wheel thickness and shape. Example: racing wheels have a narrow, V-shaped profile. Aggressive wheels have a wide, square-shaped profile.

Quad skates
Traditional roller skates with four wheels, two in front and two in back, just like the kind grandma used to wear. Wait, just like the kind *you* used to wear on the sidewalk in front of your house in the olden days.

Ramp
Structure made of metal or wood used for jumps.

Ready Position
One of the most important things to use in keeping balanced

during the bumpy times. Arms out, knees bent, the skates are parallel and wider than shoulder width.

Road Rash

A nice big purple boo boo or scrap caused by falling on your bootie, hip, or other sacred body part.

Rockering

Lowering the middle wheels to create a curved wheel line allowing the skater to make quicker turns.

Rollerblading

Like Jell-O® or Kleenex®, it is a generic term coined to refer in this case, to inline skating. It came about when the company Rollerblade® started the inline trend in the nineties and got the ball rolling, so to speak. Rollerblade® frowns upon the use of the terms like rollerblade, rollerblading, blading, and prefers for you say "inline skating" which is indeed the proper nomenclature for the sport.

Rotation

Wheels should be rotated to make them last longer and for better performance. One typically switches wheels one with three, two with four, flipping the wheel so the worn edge is on the outside of the skate. See Wheel Rotation.

Recreational

Casual skating or skate type, the "just-for-fun-and-exercise" skater. Makes up the largest portion of the skating population.

Safety gear

Wrist guards, elbow and kneepads made with reinforced plastic and foam that protect the wearer's joints and tender skin from scrapes and serious injury in a fall.

Scissor Stance

When one foot is placed in front of the other. Provides a longer wheelbase and stability in turning and braking.

Skitching

"Skate hitching" or hanging on to a moving vehicle such as a bus or taxi and letting it pull you along. This practice makes parents and Babes cringe. Many inline skating deaths have resulted from this practice.

Slalom
Weaving in and out of evenly spaced cones, lines, or volunteers. Faster version of the parallel turn.

Snell
Foundation which tests and certifies helmets to a high safety standard.

Spacer
A small plastic or metal piece in the center of the wheel that prevents bearings from touching each other.

Stair Riding
Something you will probably never do, but keep an eye on your teenage children. It is a practice where you literally ride down the steep metal rails of stairs, usually in public buildings.

Street
Style of skating in public areas includes jumping over objects and down stairs along the way.

Striding
Combination of stroking and gliding in a continuos motion.

Support Leg
The leg that balances the greater amount of weight.

Swizzles
A technique where the feet progress over the shape of a football or hourglass, with wheels never leaving the ground. Swizzles are a good way to keep control and stop rolling forward or even backward. Swizzles are also good way to tighten inner thighs.

T-Stop
A braking technique where the back leg is placed behind the front leg dragging the wheels of the back skate in the form of a "T." Race skaters and experts who have no heel brake use it. This practice wears down the wheels much faster than a brake. It is not recommended for beginners. This move takes tremendous balance and skill.

Vert

1. (Adj.) Short for vertical, refers to skating on ramps and pipes. 2. (N.) Part of riding surface in quarter or half-pipes that rises straight upward.

V-Walk

Same as duck walk used in learning how to maintain balance by walking with your toes pointed outward, heels inward, in a V-shaped position.

Wee-Babe

A child Babe.

Wheel Rotation

Something Babes do on a regular basis. Polyurethane wheels wear from the inside out due to the outward push of each stroke. Rotating wheels extends the life of wheels considerably by flipping and trading wheels one and three, two and four, on a regular basis. Wheel wear depends on surface, outside temperatures, and hardness of wheel.

Appendix C: Resources

The Babe Book lists only few resources because they change so dang much each year. These reliable resources have stuck in there through thick and thin over time, just like the Babes.

BEST OVERALL INLINE SKATING WEBSITE:

www.iisa.org   The International Inline Skating Association, as mentioned in Parts I and II of this book. The IISA is a nonprofit trade association that represents the thirty million regular inline skaters. This organization conducts educational and safety programs in inline skating and promotes the benefits and pleasures of inline skating for sport, recreation, fitness, and vitality.

BEST SPORTING INDUSTRY SITE

www.sgma.com
Sporting Goods Manufacturers Association (SGMA)
200 Castlewood Drive
North Palm Beach, FL 33148
561-842-4100
E-mail: sgma@ix.netcome.com

The Sporting Goods Manufacturers Association is the national trade association of more than 1,200 national brand producers and distributors of sport apparel, athletic footwear, fitness and sporting goods equipment. It is owner of The Super Show, the largest sports products show in the world. Its mission is to increase sports and fitness access and participation opportunities across the ages. (How Babe-like.) It has been the catalyst for promoting physical activity to those fifty and over through programs such as Active & Ageless which is a public relations campaign bringing together agencies like the United Nations, World Health Organization, AARP, The Fashion Association, Robert Wood Johnson Foundation, the International

Textile and Apparel Association, and the President's Council on Physical Fitness and Sports, to develop product, public policy and social marketing efforts dedicated to addressing the active interests of boomers and the fifty plus. This group has used the Babes on Blades to inspire the innocent public to get out there, exercise, and be the best they can be.

MOST INTERESTING WEEKLY INLINE SKATING WEB SITES

www.askaboutskating.com and its sister site, Skate GRRL at (http://www.inlineskating.about.com). Written by Kathie Fry, this site gives you up-to-the-moment inline skating events and news. It also provides a vast number of inline skating links and information. You can spend hours here and want to spend more. They are meaty sites indeed.

BEST INLINE SKATING MAGAZINE

Fitness and Speedskating Times (FASST) at http:// www.speedsk8in.com/ This publication has hung in there while many other inline skating magazines have faded over the last decade. FASST is distributed to over seventy countries. You can find it in your local Barnes and Nobel® or Borders®, Books Etc.®, and other venues. I have found it in California, plus on my Holland and Switzerland skating adventures. This publication cares about Babes and the topics that interest them. It covers the spectacular athletes and those, like Babes, who show up and think (and know) that they have conquered the world because they "dared to be there," even if it was with their T-shirts on backwards and curlers in their hair at early morning events.

BIGGEST PROMOTER OF CALIFORNIA SKATING BY A SINGLE PERSON

David Miles is California's Godfather of Skating and inventor of a long list of skating activities, programs and events in San Francisco and surrounding communities. He founded the California Outdoor Rollerskating Association (CORA) that puts on Napa to Calistoga, the one hundred miler (as seen in "Making New Friends in Skating,") San Francisco's Friday Night Skate and much more. Miles is a tireless campaigner for the sport and has been at it for two decades (http;/web.cora.org).

MOST RIGHT-ON INLINE SKATE TOUR COMPANY

Zephyr Inline Skate Tours and Camps. Take your skates and skate the world. This company provides national and international destinations plus skate camps. Contact: Allan Wright, P. O. Box 16, Red Lodge, MT 59068; 888-758-8687 or 406-446-0275; zephyrtours@bigfoot.com; www.skatetour.com; www.skatecamp.com. I highly recommend this company for an adventure of a lifetime. But hold on to your helmet. Many surprises await you.

Photography Credits:

All interior photography and artwork provided by Suzan Davis, with the exception of the following:

Photography on pages 3, 121, 122, 123, 152, 170, coins on page 156 and line art on page 86, all provided by Art Today (www.arttoday.com)

Photography on page 95, by Betty Brown

Photography on page 97, by Dan Granpton

Photography on page 98, by Stephen Brown

Art on pages 182-187, by Phil Velikan based on drawings provided by Suzan Davis.

QUESTIONS:

vi, 6, 52, 57, 58, 64, 66, 74 (top), 77, 86, 104, 105 (both), 106, 108, 109, 111, 113, 114, 116, 120, 176, 178, 179, 180, 190, 212

ABOUT THE AUTHOR

Suzan Davis is a tireless campaigner of self-esteem in women and men. Tormented her first forty years by diets and society's ghastly definition of beauty and body acceptance, the former California lobbyist rebelled. She created her own definition of a Babe, which includes virtually every one who wants to feel better about themselves, regardless of size or age. Davis' philosophy is, "It's my turn now. I'm a Babe." An International Inline Skating Association certified instructor, Davis inspired over two thousand Babes and He-Babes to strap on inline skates and reclaim their Babes within—right there on the streets of society.

Davis' humor column and assorted articles on numerous subjects have appeared in ninety countries in a wide variety of publications. She is a contributor to *Heavenly Miracles: Magical True Stories of Guardian Angels and Answered Prayers* by Miller, Lewis and Sander, William Morrow publisher, *Don't Sweat the Small Stuff Story Collection*, edited by Richard Carlson, published by Hyperion.

Davis lives and carries on in Granite Bay, California with her Wee-Babes Katelyn, Savannah and their mutt, Duke Patrick Neary. Suzan swears life begins after forty.